MVP
Microsoft®
Most Valuable
Professional

Azure Machine Learning Studio for The Non-Data Scientist

*Learn how to create experiments,
operationalize them using Excel and Angular .Net Core applications,
and create retraining programs to improve predictive results*

Michael Washington

Azure Machine Learning Studio for The Non-Data Scientist

Learn how to create experiments, operationalize them using Excel and Angular .Net Core applications, and create retraining programs to improve predictive results.

Copyright

Proofreading by Peter J. Francis,
editing@hgpublishing.com
www.hgpublishing.com

Table of Contents

Dedication

As always, for Valerie and Zachary.

Preface

Requirements

You must have a computer running Microsoft Windows with **Microsoft Visual Studio 2017** (or higher) to create the applications described in this book.

You can download the free **Visual Studio Community Edition** from https://www.visualstudio.com/vs/community/.

Chapter 1: The Author is Not a Data Scientist

Creating predictive models is no longer relegated to data scientists when you use tools such as the **Microsoft Azure Machine Learning Studio**.

Azure Machine Learning Studio is a web browser-based application that allows you to create and deploy predictive models as web services that can be consumed by custom applications and other tools such as **Microsoft Excel**.

However, the author is not a data scientist. Therefore, you do not need to be a data scientist to use this book.

You do not even need to be a computer programmer; however, if you are, it will help you understand the chapters that cover how to *operationalize* the sample predictive model, by creating an **Angular** application, and to retrain that model using **C#** code.

Why Do We Need Predictive Modeling?

Predictive modeling is used to guess the probability of an outcome, such as when a store will run out of inventory (so that the items can be reordered in time) by looking at the rate the product is being depleted. One might simply order everything ahead of time, but this needlessly ties up capital and resources that can better be used elsewhere. Also, you may end up ordering stock that may not ever be sold.

Cost savings achieved using **predictive modeling** can allow a business that uses predictions to schedule assembly workers or to produce products cheaper than their competitors. The ability to achieve these cost savings has traditionally required a business to hire expensive data scientists. However, using **Azure Machine Learning Studio,** non-data scientists now have access to these powerful tools.

For example, imagine that you own a used car dealership. You may find that you are undervaluing your car inventory and losing a lot of money in the process.

Predictive modeling uses data to forecast outcomes and to guess the probability of an outcome, given a set of input data. If the **predictive model** is supplied with the features of a used car, it can predict the sale price.

A **predictive model** is made up of a number of *predictors*. These are variables (such as vehicle make, model, horsepower, and the number of doors), that are likely to influence the **predicted result**.

Past data, which provides values for these variables, along with the actual price, are used to create a **model**. This **model** is used to predict the price of a vehicle. This information can then be leveraged to make your used car dealership more profitable.

An Introduction to Get You Started

It would take a lifetime to fully master all the elements and techniques of **predictive modeling**, **machine learning**, and data science. This book will only get you started.

However, this book will provide step-by-step instructions and examples of the entire process to create real world solutions that employ **predictive modeling**.

In this book, we will create a predictive model, and *operationalize* it by creating a **Microsoft .Net Core** application that uses the **Angular JavaScript** framework.

Finally, we will create programs that will allow you to automate the process to continually retrain the model with new data, thereby increasing its predictive accuracy.

Chapter 2: An End-To-End Azure Machine Learning Studio Application

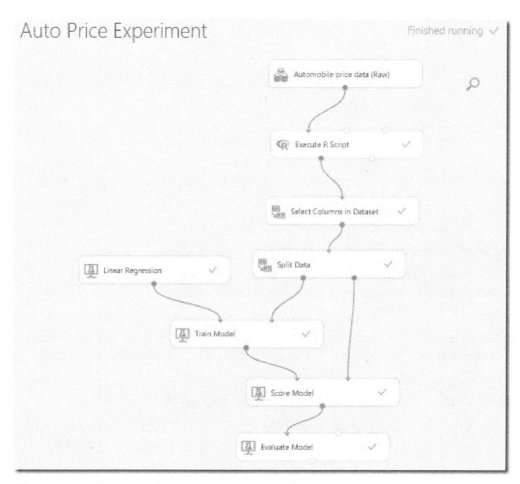

The Microsoft Azure Machine Learning Studio allows you to create complete application solutions that employ predictive analytics.

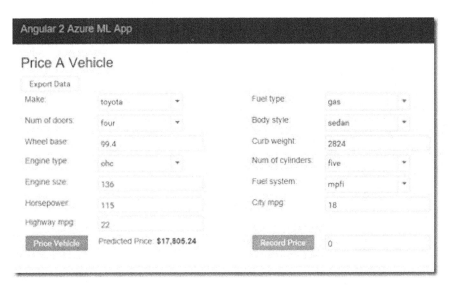

The resulting applications allow you to use data to make forecasts and predictions that drive intelligent business decisions.

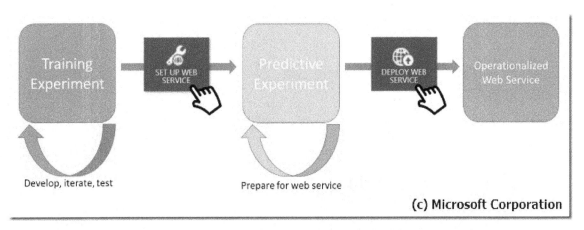

(c) Microsoft Corporation

In the following series of chapters, we will create an **Azure Machine Learning** experiment that predicts the price of a vehicle given parameters such as *make*, *horsepower*, and *body style*. It does this by creating a **Model** based on prices of previous vehicles.

We will then **operationalize the model** by creating a **web service**. We will then create an **Angular 2** application that consumes the **web service**.

Finally, we will create a programmatic method to update the model with new data gathered from our **Angular 2** application.

Create an Azure Machine Learning Workspace

If you do not already have an Azure Subscription go to: https://azure.microsoft.com/en-us/free/ to create one.

__Note:__ There is a free option to use Azure Machine Learning (simply sign in on this page). However, we will cover using the __Standard__ version that allows you to use a Free Azure Subscription. However, as you can see on the pricing page, if you do not use the Azure Machine learning too much you will not incur any significant charges. Following this demo should incur about $4 in web service charges.

Log into the **Azure Portal** (at: https://portal.azure.com/) and Click the **New** button.

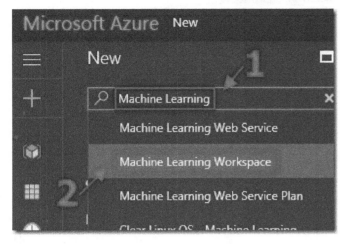

Search for Machine Learning Workspace and select it.

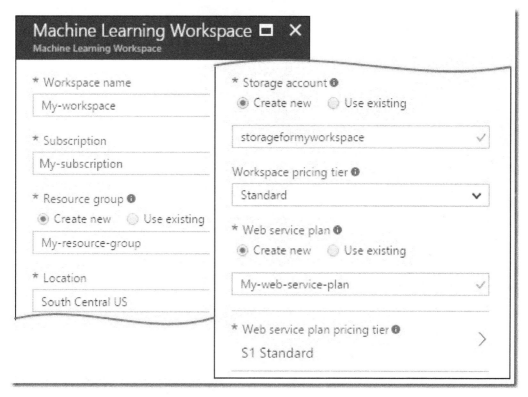

You will be guided through the wizard to create your workspace. See: Create an Azure Machine Learning workspace for documentation on the options.

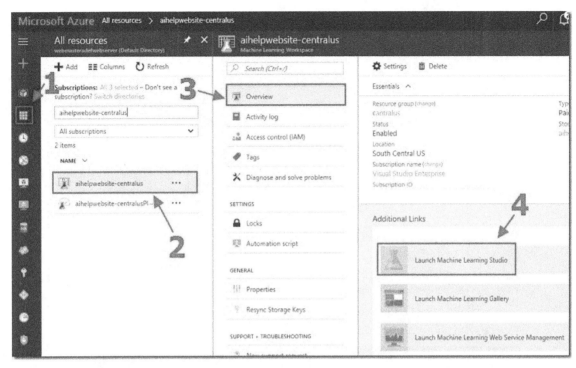

After your workspace is created, select the green **All Resources** icon, search for your **Azure Machine Learning Workspace,** and select it.

Select **Overview,** then **Launch Machine Learning Studio**.

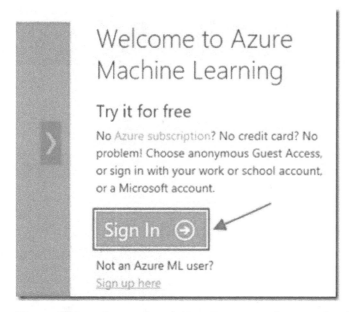

You will be taken to https://studio.azureml.net and asked to log in using your **Azure** username and password.

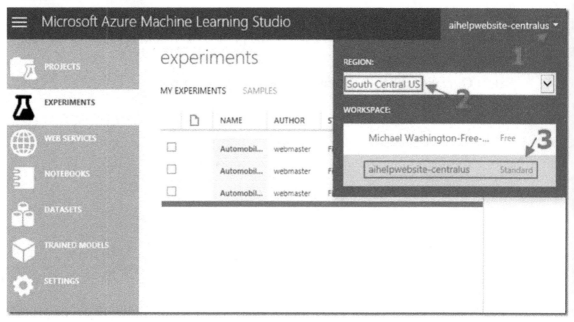

When the **Azure Machine Learning Studio** opens, ensure that you select the

Region that you created the **Workspace** in and the correct **Workspace**.

Create An Experiment

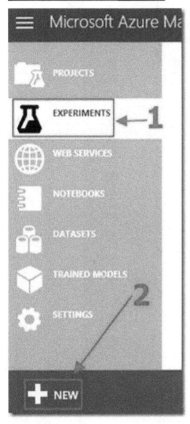

We will now create the *Auto Price Experiment*.

This will allow us to create a **Model**, evaluate it, and then *operationalize* it.

Click the **New** button.

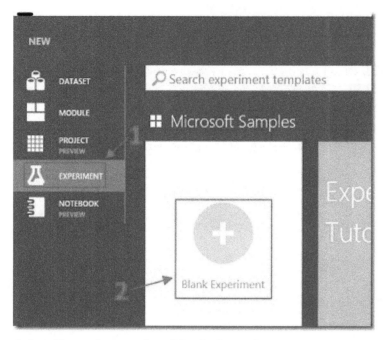

Select **Experiment,** then **Blank Experiment**.

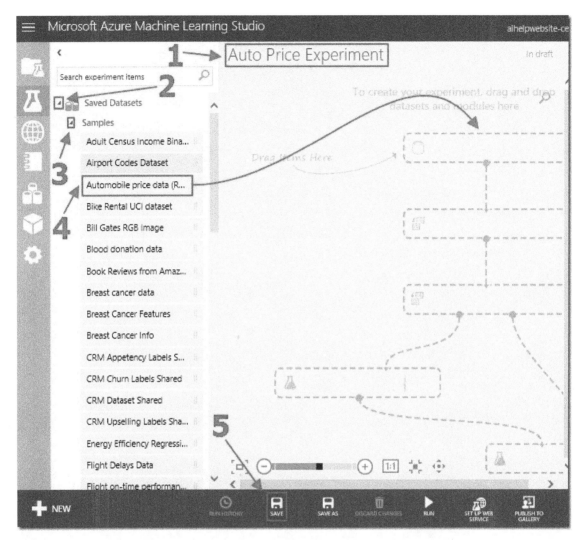

Click on the title to edit it and rename it **Auto Price Experiment**.

Expand the **Saved Datasets** node and *drag and drop* the **Automobile price data (RAW)** dataset to the design surface (the right-side of the window).

Click the **Save** button (you should click the **Save** button regularly).

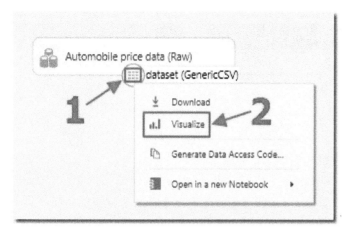

Right-click on the circle on the bottom of the **Automobile price data (RAW)** dataset and select **Visualize**.

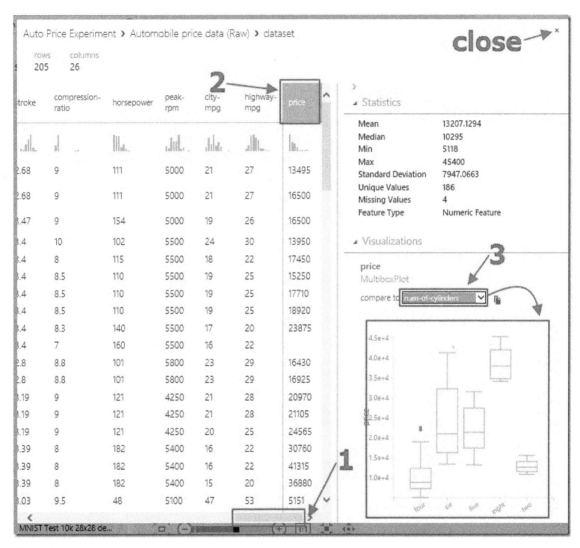

Examine the data.

For example, if you click on the **price** column and then select **num-of-cylinders** in the *compare* to box, you will see a display showing you that there is a relationship between the two that should help in building a **Model** that can make predictions.

Also, note for now there are currently **205** rows of data (see the upper left-hand corner of the window).

When you have completed the examination of the data, click the **close** button.

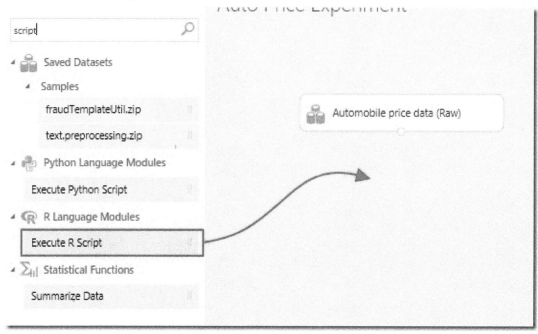

We will now demonstrate how to use an **R Script** to modify or filter data.

Search for, and *drag and drop* an **R Script** module onto the design surface.

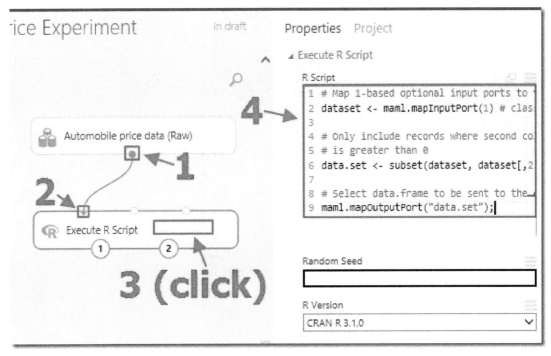

Connect the **Automobile price data (RAW)** dataset to the **Execute R Script** module by first clicking in the circle on the **Automobile price data (RAW)** dataset, and holding the mouse button down as you drag to the left circle on top of the **Execute R Script** module. Then let the mouse button go.

You may have to try a few times until you get the hang of it.

Click on the **Execute R Script module** to select it.

Paste the following script in the **R Script** box:

```
# Map 1-based optional input ports to variables
dataset <- maml.mapInputPort(1) # class: data.frame
# Only include records where second column (normalized-losses)
# is greater than 0
data.set <- subset(dataset, dataset[,2] > 0)
# Select data.frame to be sent to the output Dataset port
maml.mapOutputPort("data.set");
```

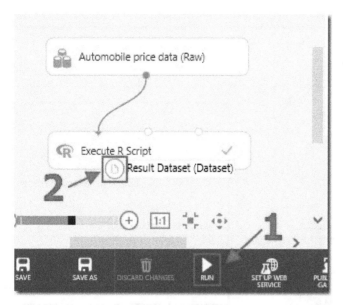

Click the **Run** button to populate data from the **Automobile price data (RAW)** dataset to the **Execute R Script** module.

After the data has been populated (you will know it is complete because you will see a green checkbox on the **Execute R Script** module), *right-click* on the bottom left-hand circle on the **Execute R Script** module and select **Visualize**.

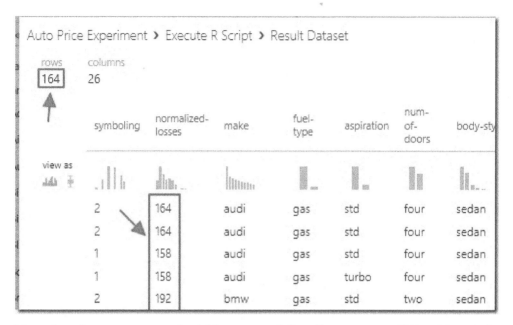

Note that there are now only **164** rows, and for all rows, **normalized-losses** is greater than **0**.

Select Columns

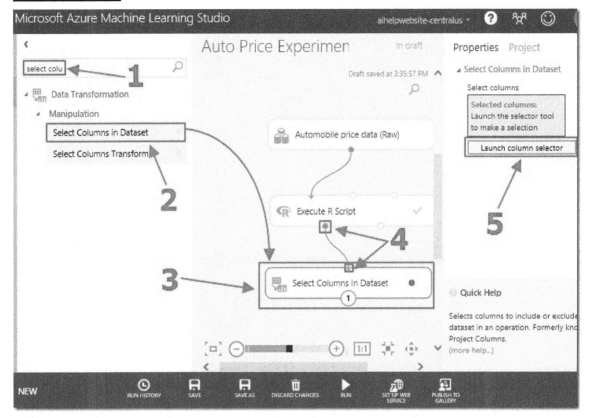

We only want to include the columns that will benefit the **Model**.

Search for the **Select Columns in Dataset** module and *drag it* onto the design surface.

Connect it to the **Execute R Script** module.

While the **Select Columns in Dataset** module is selected, click the **Launch column selector** button.

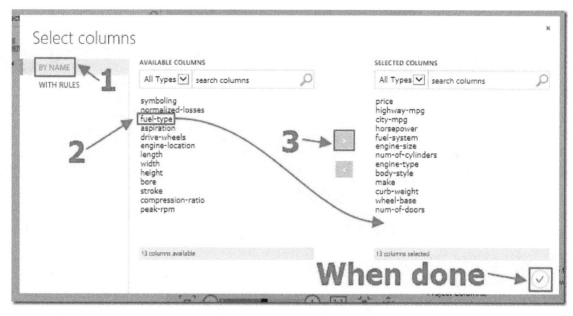

Select each column from **Available Columns** and move it to the **Selected Columns** section by clicking the right pointing arrow button (after selecting each column).

Add the following columns:

- price
- highway-mpg
- city-mpg
- horsepower
- fuel-system
- engine-size
- num-of-cylinders
- engine-type
- body-style
- make
- curb-weight
- wheel-base
- num-of-doors
- fuel-type

Click the check box in the lower *right-hand* corner when done to close the window.

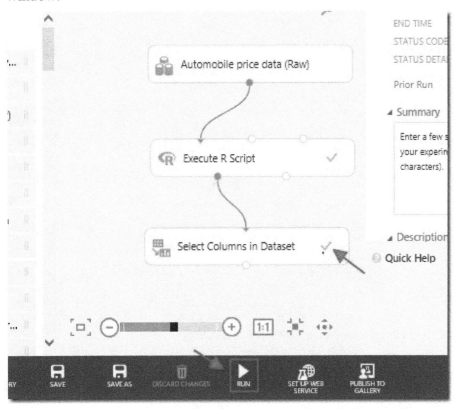

Click the **Run** button to populate the data into the **Select Columns in Dataset** module.

A green check will appear in the module when the process is complete.

Split Data

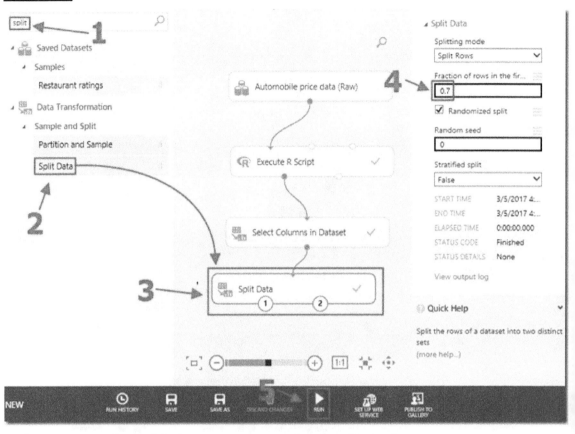

Before we can train the **Model**, we need to randomly split the data.

Part of the data will be used for training the **Model**, and the other *held back* data will be used to *validate* the **Model**.

Drag and drop a **Split Data** module to the design surface and connect it to the **Select Columns in Dataset** module.

While the **Select Columns in Dataset** module is selected, set the **Fraction of rows in the first output dataset** to **0.7** (to indicate that **70%** of the data will be used to train the **Model**).

Click **Run** to populate the data to the module.

Train The Model

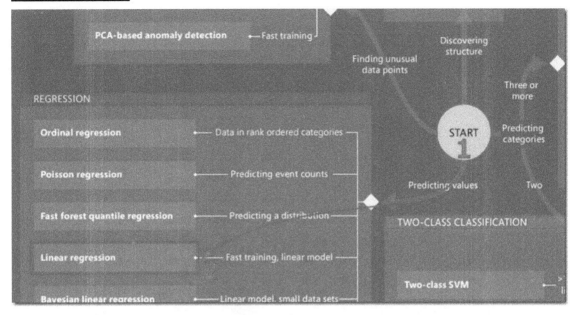

We now need to pick a **Model** to train.

Consult Machine learning algorithm cheat sheet (https://docs.microsoft.com/en-us/azure/machine-learning/machine-learning-algorithm-cheat-sheet) and How to choose algorithms for Microsoft Azure Machine Learning (https://docs.microsoft.com/en-us/azure/machine-learning/machine-learning-algorithm-choice) to determine a **Model** to use.

Doing this, we decide to train a *Linear Regression* **Model**.

Note, we would normally try different **Models** and different settings to determine the best one to use.

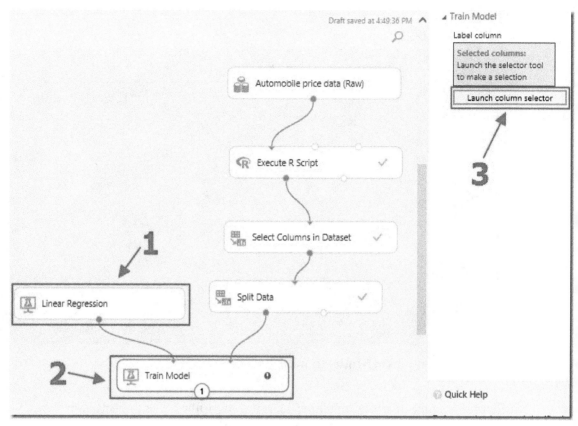

Drag and drop a **Linear Regression** module and a **Train Model** module onto the design surface, and connect them together along with the **Split Data** module.

While the **Train Model** module is selected, click the **Launch column selector** button.

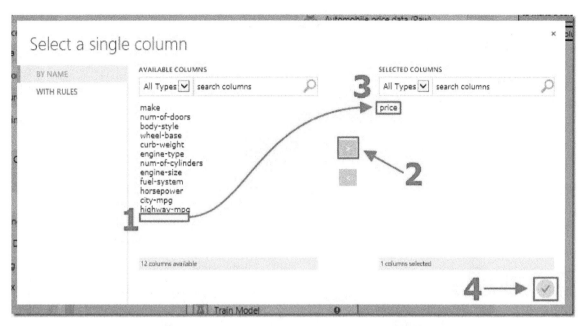

Select the **price** column, because it is the column that we want the **Model** to *predict*.

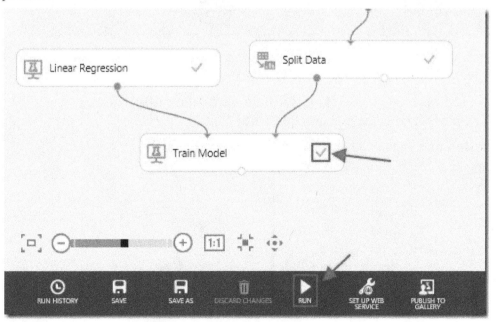

Click **Run** to populate the data into the **Train Model** module.

Score The Model

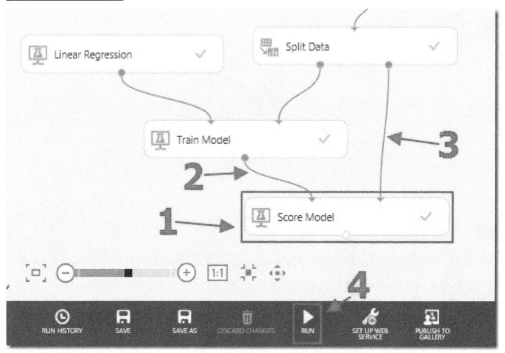

We now need to score the **Model** against the data held back with the **Split Data** module.

Drag and drop a **Score Model** module onto the design surface, and connect it to the **Train Model** module and the **Split Data** module.

Click **Run** to populate the data into the **Score Model** module.

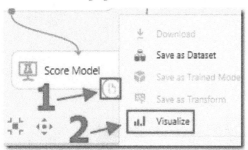

Visualize the **Score Model** results.

rows   columns
49   14

engine-size	fuel-system	horsepower	city-mpg	highway-mpg	price	Scored Labels
136	mpfi	115	18	22	17450	20620.916973
171	mpfi	156	20	24	15690	17333.289988
90	2bbl	70	38	43	6295	6653.824383
146	mpfi	116	24	30	11549	11093.314206
70	4bbl	101	17	23	11845	10947.695456
183	idi	123	22	25	31600	30947.281611
70	4bbl	101	17	23	13645	10968.605381
110	idi	73	30	33	10698	9916.372172
122	mpfi	92	29	34	8948	9695.436396
98	2bbl	70	30	37	6938	7120.856463
110	1bbl	86	27	33	10295	9311.073356
91	2bbl	68	31	38	6795	8294.661094

When we look at the last two columns, we can see the actual price in the **price** column, and the price that the **Model** predicted in the **Scored Labels** column.

Evaluate The Model

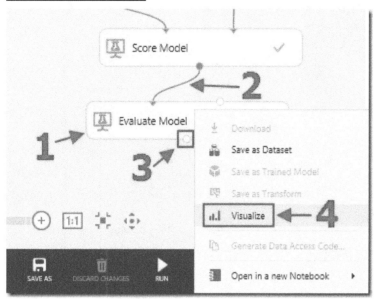

We now need to *evaluate* the performance of the **Model**.

Drag and drop an **Evaluate Model** module onto the design surface, and connect it to the **Score Model** module.

Click **Run** to populate the data into the **Evaluate Model** module.

Right-click on the bottom left-hand circle on the **Evaluate Model** module and select **Visualize**.

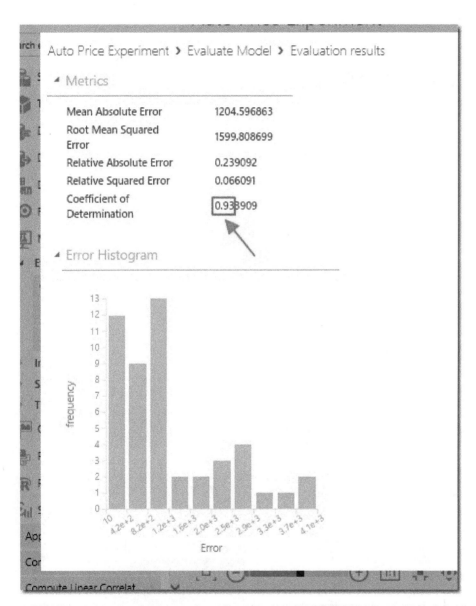

To fully understand the results of an evaluation, see: How to evaluate model performance in Azure Machine Learning (**https://docs.microsoft.com/en-us/azure/machine-learning/machine-learning-evaluate-model-performance**)

For a Linear Regression, a Coefficient of Determination of **0.93** (**1.0** is the highest possible value) is considered excellent.

Save the experiment.

Create A Predictive Web Service

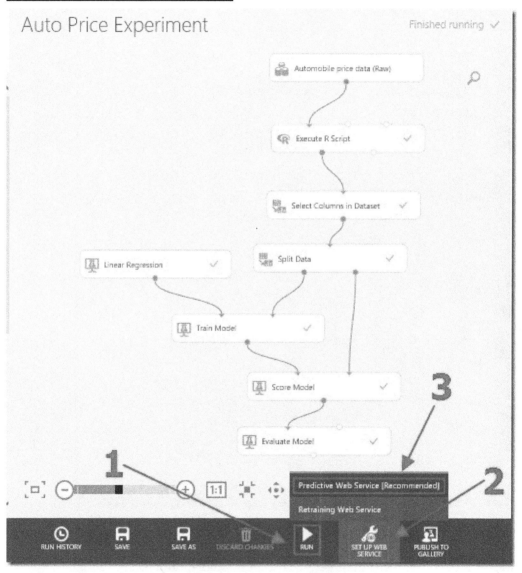

Now that we have a **Model**, we need to *operationalize* it (turn it into something that we can consume).

Click **Run** to run the entire experiment (you must do this step or the option to create a **Predictive Web Service** will not be available).

Click the **Set Up Web Service** button and select **Predictive Web Service**.

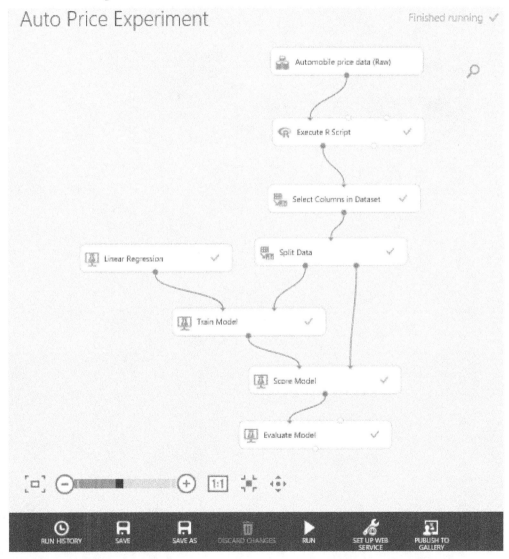

The **Predictive Experiment** will be created.

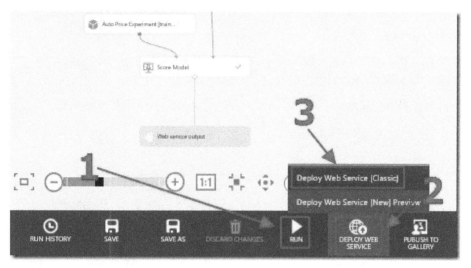

Click the **Run** button to *run* and validate the **Predictive Experiment**.

Click the **Deploy Web Service** button and select **Deploy Web Service [Classic]**.

Consume The Model Using Excel

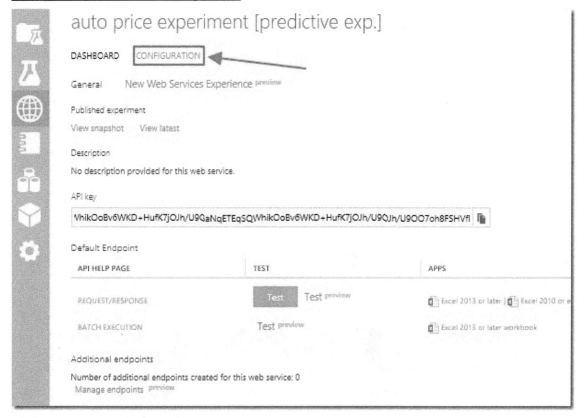

We now have a **web service** that can be consumed programmatically.

However, it helps to enable the *sample data* option when consuming the **web service** in **Microsoft Excel**.

Click the **Configuration** button.

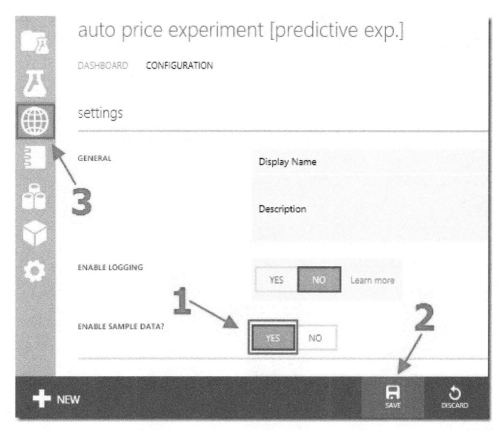

Click the **Yes** button next to **Enable Sample Data** and then click the **Save** button.

Click the *world icon* to navigate to the menu that will show all your web services.

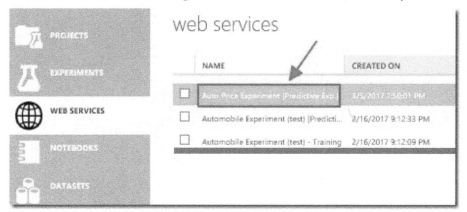

This is the menu that allows you to return to your **web services** at any time.

In the list of **web services**, click on the **web service** you were working on to return to its *configuration*.

Click on the **Excel 2013 or later** link on the **Request/Response** row.

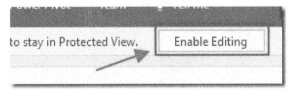

Save the **Excel** file that will pop up, and open it in **Microsoft Excel**.

When you open the file in **Microsoft Excel**, you will have to **Enable Editing**.

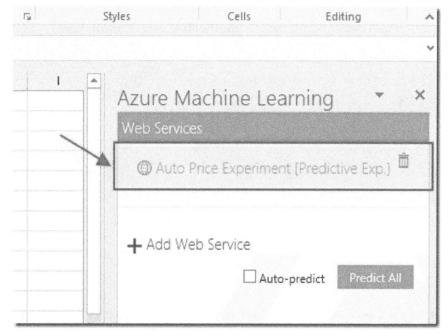

The **Machine Learning** *plug-in* will display.

Click the button that has the name of the experiment to enable it.

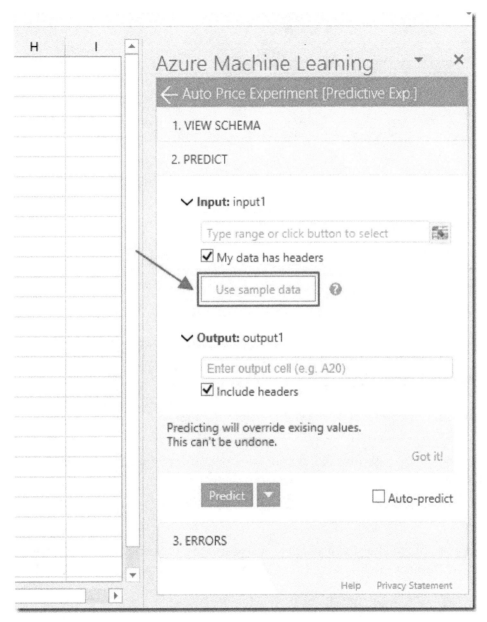

Click the **Use sample data** button.

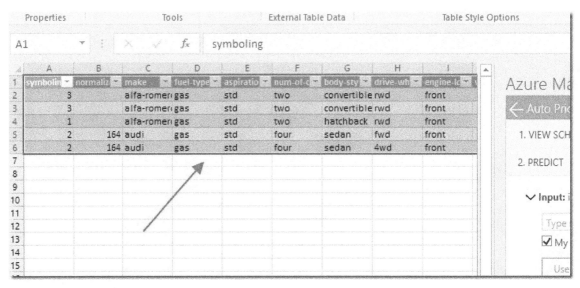

Sample data will display.

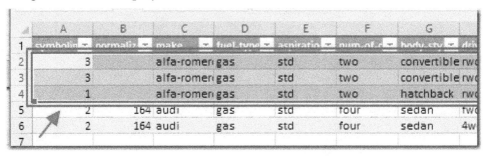

Highlight and *delete* any rows that do not have data for all columns. Otherwise this will cause an error.

The **web service** expects a value for all fields even if they are not all used by the final **Model**.

Note, it is possible to alter the predictive **web service** by adding a **Select Columns in Dataset** module to only require values that are used by the **Model**.

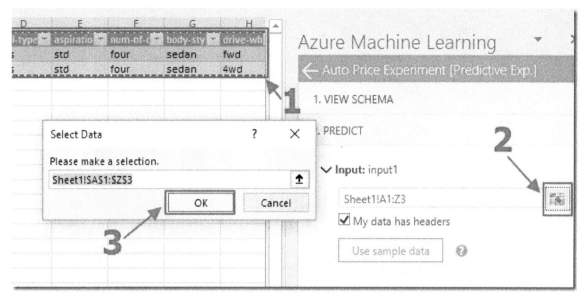

Highlight the remaining sample data. *Click* the **cell selection button** next to **Input**. The cells should now be selected in the **Select Data** popup.

Click the **Ok** button.

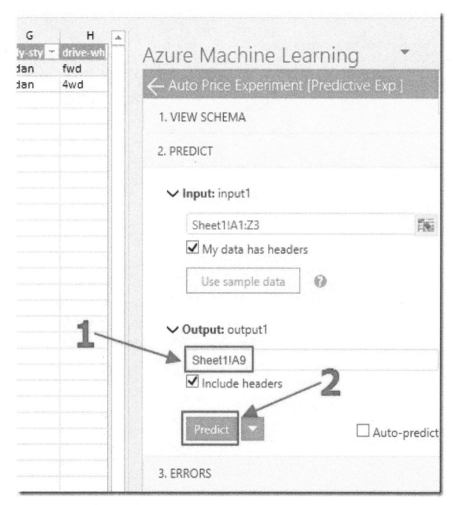

Enter a cell for an open row on the **Excel** sheet under **Output** and click the **Predict** button.

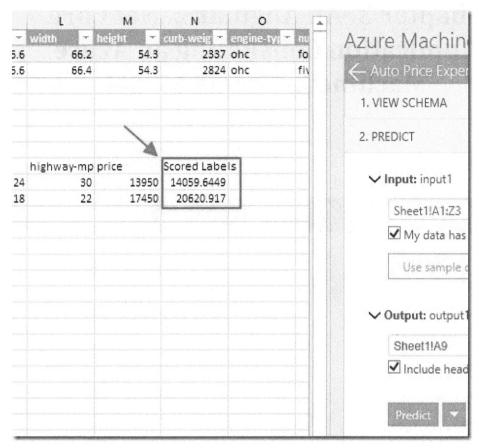

The **web service**, in **Azure**, will be called and will pass the sample values to the **Model**.

The **Model** will return the predicted value for the **price**.

The **Scored Labels** section will contain the price predicted by the **Model**.

Chapter 3: An Angular 2 .Net Core Application Consuming an Azure Machine Learning Model

(The code for the following chapter is available at the link: An Angular 2+ .Net Core Application Consuming an Azure Machine Learning Model at http://aihelpwebsite.com/Downloads)

You can create an Angular 2 application that consumes a web service created from an Azure Machine Learning experiment.

In the preceding chapter, we created an **Azure Machine Learning** experiment that predicts the price of a vehicle given parameters such as *make*, *horsepower*, and *body style*. We then operationalized the model by creating a **web service**.

In this chapter, we will create an **Angular 2** application that consumes the **web**

service. In the next chapter, we will create a programmatic method to update the model with new data gathered from our **Angular 2** application.

The Application

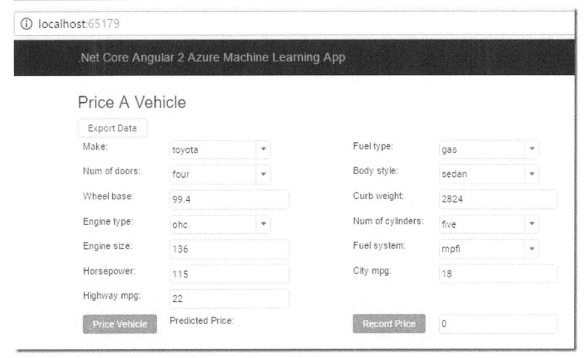

The application, covered in this chapter, allows users to set the values that will be passed to the **Azure Machine Learning** web service (that was created in the previous chapter).

The user can click the **Price Vehicle** button to call the web service.

The **Predicted Price**, returned by the web service, will then display.

The user can also record the actual sale price (based on the currently selected values) by entering the value and clicking the **Record Price** button.

The data will be stored in the local database file.

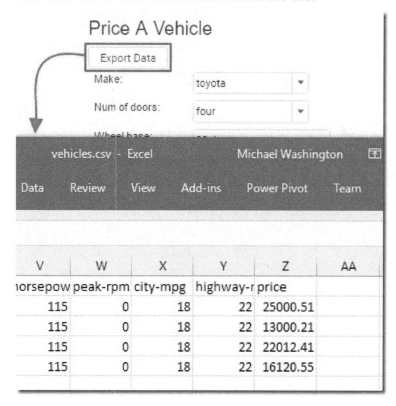

Clicking the **Export Data** button will produce a **.csv** file that can then be used to retrain the **Azure Machine Learning Model**, thereby improving the future predictions.

Creating The Application

If you do not already have them, install the following prerequisites:

- Visual Studio 2017
- Node.js (version 6 or later)

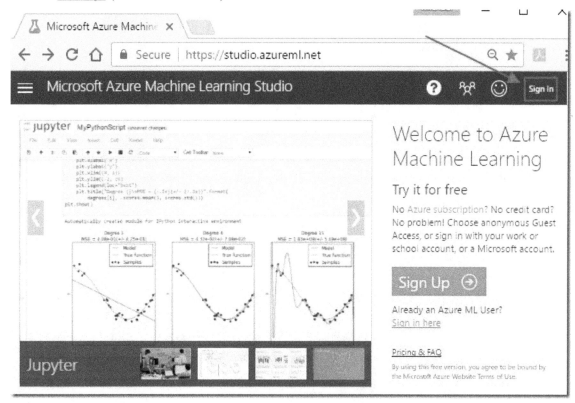

Log into the **Azure Machine Learning Studio** at: https://studio.azureml.net/.

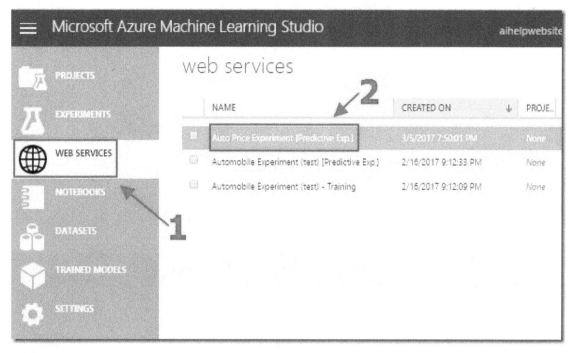

Select **Web Services**, then the *predictive* web service that we created in the previous chapter.

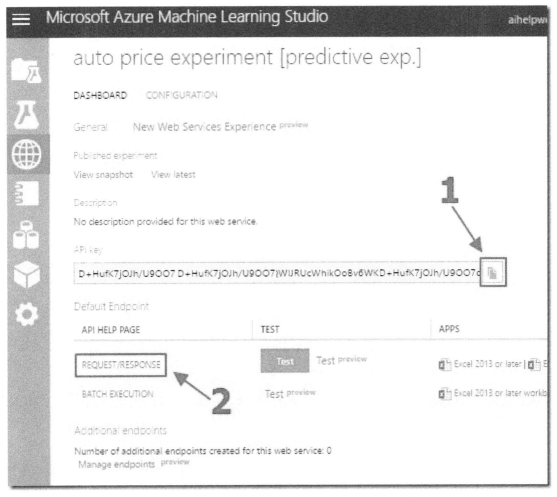

1) **Click** the button to copy the **API Key**. Save it. We will need it later. This will be what we will use as the **PrimaryKey** value in the **appsettings.json** file.

2) **Click** the **REQUEST/RESPONSE** link that will take us to the sample code page.

Request Response API Documentation for Auto Price Experir [Predictive Exp.]

Updated: 03/06/2017 03:50

No description provided for this web service.

- Previous version of this API
- Submit a request
- Input Parameters
- Output Parameters
- Web App Template for RRS
- Sample Code
- API Swagger Document
- Endpoint Managment Swagger Document

Request

Method	Request URI
POST	https://ussouthcentral.services.azureml.net/workspaces/4e2f7050438a47eb8ebde5e3b0986072/services/05ba2b7006874c9 18aa34c7ea84d8d0e/execute?api-version=2.0&details=true

Note: You may omit the **details** parameter from the query string. This would cause **ColumnTypes** to be omitted from the output

When the **Request Response API Documentation** page displays, copy the **Request POST** web address. Save it. We will need it later.

This will be what we will use as the **BaseAddress** value in the **appsettings.json** file.

Sample Code

C#	Python	R

```
// This code requires the Nuget package Microsoft.AspNet.WebApi.Client to be installed.
// Instructions for doing this in Visual Studio:
// Tools -> Nuget Package Manager -> Package Manager Console
// Install-Package Microsoft.AspNet.WebApi.Client

using System;
using System.Collections.Generic;
using System.IO;
using System.Net.Http;
using System.Net.Http.Formatting;
using System.Net.Http.Headers;
using System.Text;
using System.Threading.Tasks;

namespace CallRequestResponseService
{

    public class StringTable
    {
        public string[] ColumnNames { get; set; }
        public string[,] Values { get; set; }
```

Next, scroll down to the bottom of the page to see sample code that calls the web service.

This is what we will use at the base code for our application.

Create The .Net Core Application

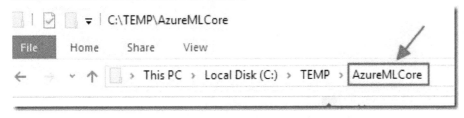

Create a **folder** on your **Microsoft Windows** computer (this tutorial was created

57

using **Windows 10**).

Note: Do not have any *special characters* in the folder name. For example, an exclamation mark (!) will break the **JavaScript** code.

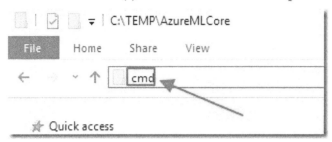

You can type **CMD** and press **Enter** to switch to the command line (and still be in that directory).

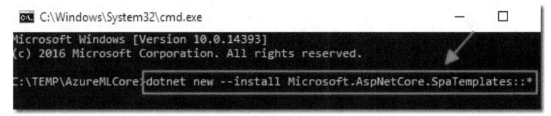

If you have not already installed JavaScriptServices (https://blogs.msdn.microsoft.com/webdev/2017/02/14/building-single-page-applications-on-asp-net-core-with-javascriptservices) install them by entering (and pressing **Enter**):

```
dotnet new --install Microsoft.AspNetCore.SpaTemplates::*
```

```
Templates                                    Short Name     Language      Tags
--------------------------------------------------------------------------------
Console Application                          console        [C#], F#      Common/Console
Class library                                classlib       [C#], F#      Common/Library
Unit Test Project                            mstest         [C#], F#      Test/MSTest
xUnit Test Project                           xunit          [C#], F#      Test/xUnit
ASP.NET Core Empty                           web            [C#]          Web/Empty
ASP.NET Core Web App                         mvc            [C#], F#      Web/MVC
MVC ASP.NET Core with Angular                angular        [C#]          Web/MVC/SPA
MVC ASP.NET Core with Aurelia                aurelia        [C#]          Web/MVC/SPA
MVC ASP.NET Core with Knockout.js            knockout       [C#]          Web/MVC/SPA
MVC ASP.NET Core with React.js               react          [C#]          Web/MVC/SPA
MVC ASP.NET Core with React.js and Redux     reactredux     [C#]          Web/MVC/SPA
ASP.NET Core Web API                         webapi         [C#]          Web/WebAPI
Solution File                                sln                          Solution

Examples:
    dotnet new mvc --auth None --framework netcoreapp1.1
    dotnet new classlib
    dotnet new --help
```

The screen display will indicate the templates now available.

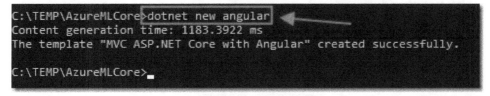

Create the **ASP.NET Core JavaScriptServices** application by entering (and pressing **Enter**):

```
dotnet new angular
```

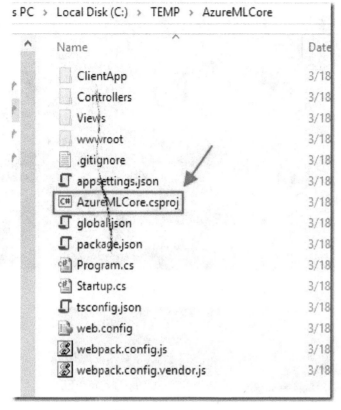

The application will be created.

Double-click on the ***.csproj** file to open it in **Visual Studio 2017**.

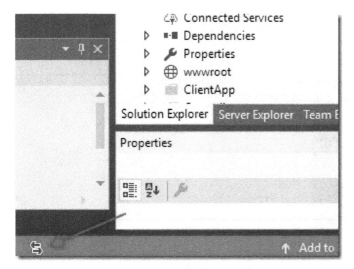

Visual Studio will start restoring **.Net** dependencies and the node_modules (you can view the **node_modules** in the file explorer to see the items populated).

(Note: This can take 3-10 minutes or more.)

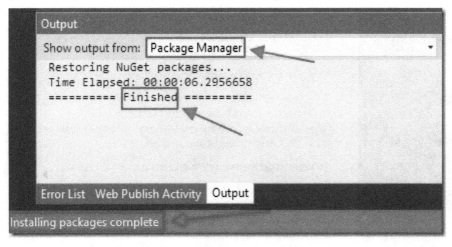

Visual Studio will indicate when everything is complete.

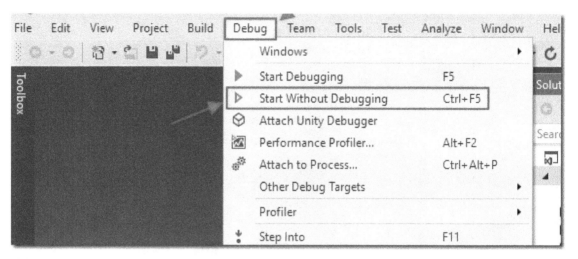

Press **Ctrl+F5** to **Start Without Debugging**.

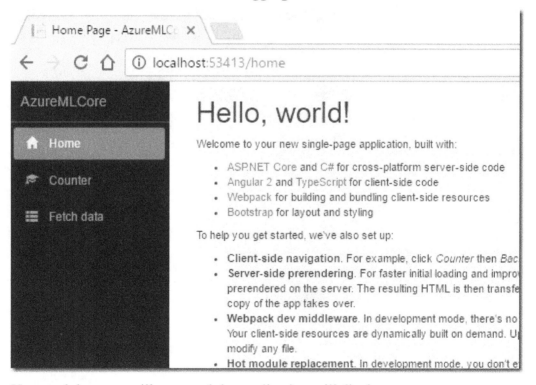

Your web browser will open and the application will display.

Close the web browser for now.

Add PrimeNG

We will now install the free open source PrimeNG **Angular 2** components.

```
  preboot : 4.3.2,
  "raw-loader": "^0.5.1",
  "rxjs": "^5.0.1",
  "style-loader": "^0.13.1",
  "to-string-loader": "^1.1.5",
  "typescript": "^2.2.1",
  "url-loader": "^0.5.7",
  "webpack": "^2.2.0",
  "webpack-hot-middleware": "^2.12.2",
  "webpack-merge": "^0.14.1",
  "zone.js": "^0.7.6",
  "font-awesome": "^4.7.0",
  "primeng": "^2.0.0"
},
  "devDependencies": {
  "@types/chai": "^3.4.34",
  "@types/jasmine": "^2.5.37",
  "chai": "^3.5.0",
  "jasmine-core": "^2.5.2".
```

```
              Connected Service
▷  ■-■ Dependencies
▷  🔧 Properties
▷  ⊕ wwwroot
▷     ClientApp
▷     Controllers
▷     Views
      📄 .gitignore
      🎴 appsettings.json
      🎴 global.json
      🎴 package.json
▷  C# Program.cs
▷  C# Startup.cs
      🎴 tsconfig.json
      🎴 web.config
▷  🎴 webpack.config.js
```

Open the **package.json** file and add:

```
"font-awesome": "^4.7.0",
"primeng": "^2.0.0"
```

Save the file.

```
        ]
    },
    entry: {
        vendor: [
            '@angular/common',
            '@angular/compiler',
            '@angular/core',
            '@angular/http',
            '@angular/platform-browser',
            '@angular/platform-browser-dynamic',
            '@angular/router',
            '@angular/platform-server',
            'angular2-universal',
            'angular2-universal-polyfills',
            'bootstrap',
            'bootstrap/dist/css/bootstrap.css',
            'es6-shim',
            'es6-promise',
            'event-source-polyfill',
            'jquery',
            'font-awesome/css/font-awesome.css',
            'primeng/primeng',
            'primeng/resources/themes/omega/theme.css',
            'primeng/resources/primeng.min.css',
            'zone.js'
```

Search Solution Explorer (Ctrl+;)

- Solution 'AzureMLCore' (1 project)
  - **AzureMLCore**
    - Connected Services
    - ▷ Dependencies
    - ▷ Properties
    - ▷ wwwroot
    - ▷ ClientApp
    - ▷ Controllers
    - ▷ Views
    - .gitignore
    - appsettings.json
    - global.json
    - package.json
    - ▷ C# Program.cs
    - ▷ C# Startup.cs
    - tsconfig.json
    - web.config
    - webpack.config.js
      - webpack.config.vendor.js

Open the **webpack.config.vendor.js** file and add:

```
'font-awesome/css/font-awesome.css',
'primeng/primeng',
'primeng/resources/themes/omega/theme.css',
'primeng/resources/primeng.min.css',
```

```
module.exports = (env) => {
    const extractCSS = new ExtractTextPlugin(
    const isDevBuild = !(env && env.prod);
    const sharedConfig = {
        stats: { modules: false },
        resolve: { extensions: [ '.js' ] },
        module: {
            rules: [
                { test: /\.(png|gif|woff|woff
            ]
        },
        entry: {
            vendor: [
                '@angular/common',
```

Also, in *rules/test*, add:

```
|gif
```

Save the file.

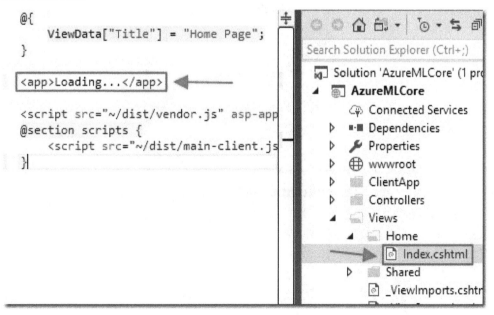

At this time, **PrimeNg** does not support pre-rendering so in

65

..\Views\Home\Index.cshtml, change:

```
<app asp-prerender-module="ClientApp/dist/main-server">Loading...</app>
```

to:

```
<app>Loading...</app>
```

Save the file.

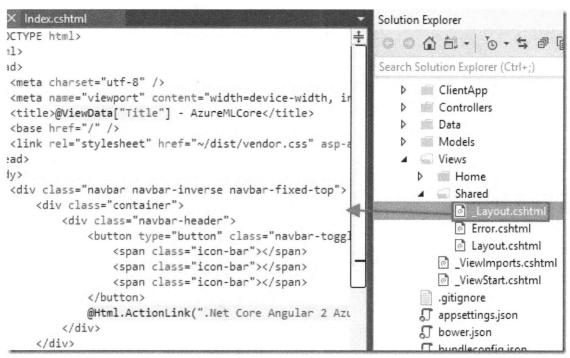

Open **..\Views\Shared_Layout.cshtml** and replace all the code with the following code:

```
<!DOCTYPE html>
<html>
<head>
    <meta charset="utf-8" />
    <meta name="viewport" content="width=device-width, initial-scale=1.0" />
    <title>@ViewData["Title"] - AzureMLCore</title>
    <base href="/" />
    <link rel="stylesheet" href="~/dist/vendor.css" asp-append-version="true" />
</head>
<body>
    <div class="navbar navbar-inverse navbar-fixed-top">
        <div class="container">
            <div class="navbar-header">
                <button type="button" class="navbar-toggle"
                        data-toggle="collapse" data-target=".navbar-collapse">
                    <span class="icon-bar"></span>
                    <span class="icon-bar"></span>
                    <span class="icon-bar"></span>
                </button>
                @Html.ActionLink(".Net Core Angular 2 Azure Machine Learning App",
                "Index", "Home", new { area = "" }, new { @class = "navbar-brand" })
            </div>
        </div>
    </div>
    <div class="container body-content">
        @RenderBody()
    </div>
    <hr />
    @RenderSection("scripts", required: false)
</body>
</html>
```

```
C:\Windows\System32\cmd.exe                                        —    □

C:\TEMP\AzureMLCore>webpack --config webpack.config.vendor.js
Hash: 334e7a7cf796b7a32a03d465f92d6dd6b76103c8
Version: webpack 2.2.1
Child
    Hash: 334e7a7cf796b7a32a03
    Time: 12706ms
                                  Asset    Size  Chunks                     Chunk Names
    674f50d287a8c48dc19ba404d20fe713.eot   166 kB          [emitted]
    912ec66d7572ff821749319396470bde.svg   444 kB          [emitted]  [big]
    b06871f281fee6b241d60582ae9369b9.ttf   166 kB          [emitted]
    89889688147bd7575d6327160d64e760.svg   109 kB          [emitted]
                              vendor.js  5.84 MB       0   [emitted]  [big]  vendor
                             vendor.css   921 kB       0   [emitted]  [big]  vendor
Child
    Hash: d465f92d6dd6b76103c8
    Time: 10633ms
                                  Asset    Size  Chunks                     Chunk Names
    89889688147bd7575d6327160d64e760.svg   109 kB          [emitted]
    674f50d287a8c48dc19ba404d20fe713.eot   166 kB          [emitted]
    912ec66d7572ff821749319396470bde.svg   444 kB          [emitted]  [big]
    b06871f281fee6b241d60582ae9369b9.ttf   166 kB          [emitted]
                              vendor.js  5.69 MB       0   [emitted]  [big]  vendor
C:\TEMP\AzureMLCore>
```

We altered the **webpack.config.vendor.js** file (to add **PrimeNg** and Font Awesome) but the compiled files that it creates (that are used at *runtime*) are not updated by the normal build process. We have to run its configuration manually whenever we alter it.

In a command prompt, at the project root, run:

```
webpack --config webpack.config.vendor.js
```

(**Note:** If you don't already have the webpack tool installed (for example you get an error when you run the code above), you'll need to run: **npm install -g webpack** first).

Add The Database

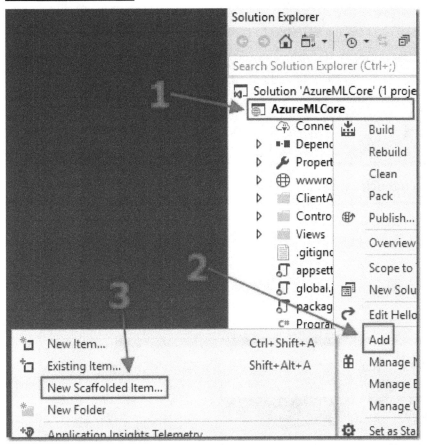

Right-click on the project node, select **Add,** then **New Scaffolded Item…**

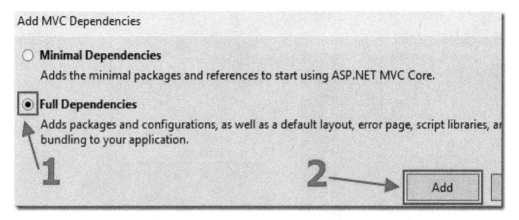

Select **Full Dependencies** then click **Add**.

The **Scaffolding** will run.

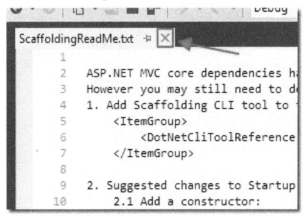

Close the **ScaffoldingReadMe.txt** file that opens.

We will perform the needed changes it describes in the next steps.

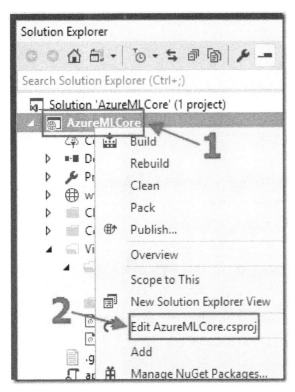

Right-click on the project node and select **Edit AzureMLCore.csproj**.

```
AzureMLCore.csproj  ⊕ X
  1 ⊟<Project ToolsVersion="15.0" Sdk="Microsoft.NET.Sdk.Web">
  2 ⊟  <PropertyGroup>
  3      <TargetFramework>netcoreapp1.1</TargetFramework>
  4      <TypeScriptCompileBlocked>true</TypeScriptCompileBlocked>
  5      <PackageTargetFallback>$(PackageTargetFallback);portable-net45+win8+wp8+wpa81;</PackageTargetFallback
  6    </PropertyGroup>
  7 ⊟  <ItemGroup>
  8      <PackageReference Include="Microsoft.AspNetCore" Version="1.1.1" />
  9      <PackageReference Include="Microsoft.AspNetCore.Mvc" Version="1.1.2" />
 10      <PackageReference Include="Microsoft.AspNetCore.SpaServices" Version="1.1.0" />
 11      <PackageReference Include="Microsoft.AspNetCore.StaticFiles" Version="1.1.1" />
 12      <PackageReference Include="Microsoft.EntityFrameworkCore.Design" Version="1.1.1" />
 13      <PackageReference Include="Microsoft.EntityFrameworkCore.SqlServer" Version="1.1.1" />
 14      <PackageReference Include="Microsoft.EntityFrameworkCore.SqlServer.Design" Version="1.1.1" />
 15      <PackageReference Include="Microsoft.Extensions.Logging.Debug" Version="1.1.1" />
 16      <PackageReference Include="Microsoft.VisualStudio.Web.BrowserLink" Version="1.1.0" />
 17      <PackageReference Include="Microsoft.VisualStudio.Web.CodeGeneration.Design" Version="1.1.0" />
 18      <DotNetCliToolReference Include="Microsoft.VisualStudio.Web.CodeGeneration.Tools" Version="1.0.0" />
 19    </ItemGroup>
```

Add:

71

```
<DotNetCliToolReference Include="Microsoft.VisualStudio.Web.CodeGeneration.Tools" Version="1.0.0" />
```

Save and **close** the file.

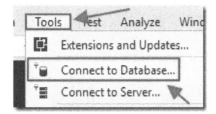

From the menu in **Visual Studio**, select **Tools,** then **Connect to Database…**

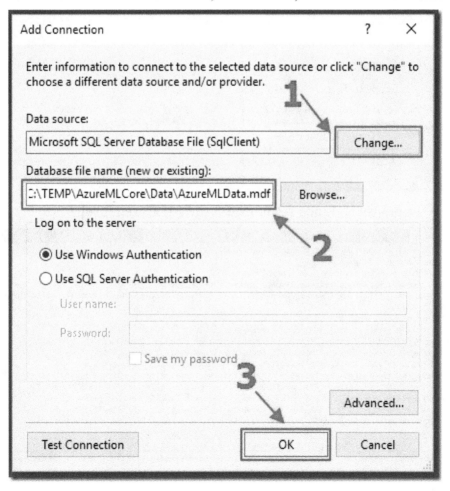

Ensure that **Microsoft SQL Server Database File (SqlClient)** is selected for **Data source** (use the **Change** button if not).

Enter **AzureMLData.mdf** for the database name and indicate that it is in a folder called *Data* that is under your project root (the file does not yet exist, so it will be created by **Visual Studio**).

Click **OK.**

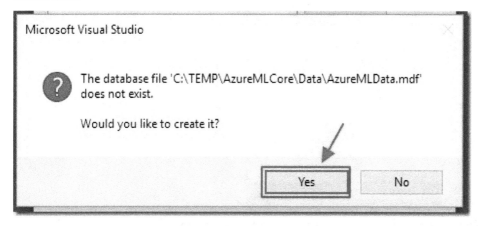

When the confirmation box appears, click **Yes** to create the database.

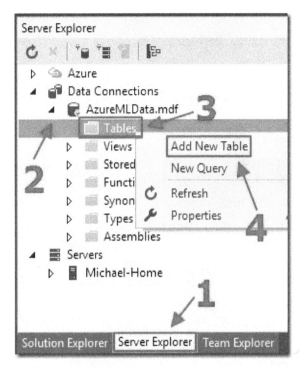

In the **Server Explorer** window in **Visual Studio** (you can get to it from the **Visual Studio** menu using **View** then **Server Explorer**), the database will show.

Expand it, *right-click* on the **Tables** node and select **Add New Table**.

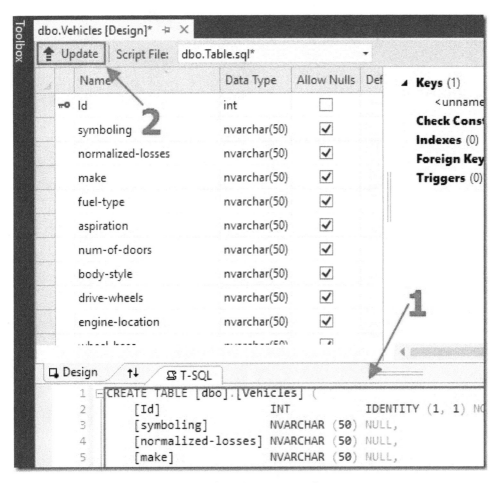

Enter the following script and click the **Update** button:

```
CREATE TABLE [dbo].[Vehicles] (
    [Id]                  INT          IDENTITY (1, 1) NOT NULL,
    [symboling]           NVARCHAR (50) NULL,
    [normalized-losses]   NVARCHAR (50) NULL,
    [make]                NVARCHAR (50) NULL,
    [fuel-type]           NVARCHAR (50) NULL,
    [aspiration]          NVARCHAR (50) NULL,
    [num-of-doors]        NVARCHAR (50) NULL,
    [body-style]          NVARCHAR (50) NULL,
    [drive-wheels]        NVARCHAR (50) NULL,
    [engine-location]     NVARCHAR (50) NULL,
    [wheel-base]          NVARCHAR (50) NULL,
    [length]              NVARCHAR (50) NULL,
    [width]               NVARCHAR (50) NULL,
    [height]              NVARCHAR (50) NULL,
    [curb-weight]         NVARCHAR (50) NULL,
    [engine-type]         NVARCHAR (50) NULL,
    [num-of-cylinders]    NVARCHAR (50) NULL,
    [engine-size]         NVARCHAR (50) NULL,
    [fuel-system]         NVARCHAR (50) NULL,
    [bore]                NVARCHAR (50) NULL,
    [stroke]              NVARCHAR (50) NULL,
    [compression-ratio]   NVARCHAR (50) NULL,
    [horsepower]          NVARCHAR (50) NULL,
    [peak-rpm]            NVARCHAR (50) NULL,
    [city-mpg]            NVARCHAR (50) NULL,
    [highway-mpg]         NVARCHAR (50) NULL,
    [price]               NVARCHAR (50) NULL,
    PRIMARY KEY CLUSTERED ([Id] ASC)
);
```

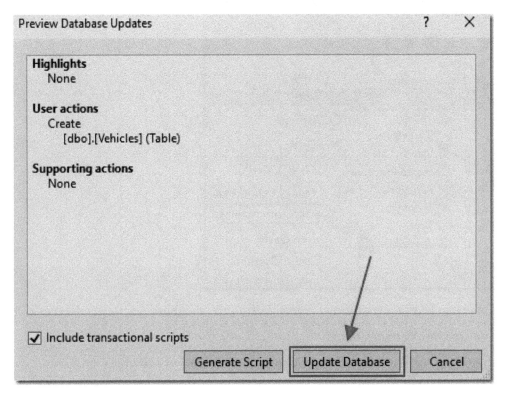

Click **Update Database**.

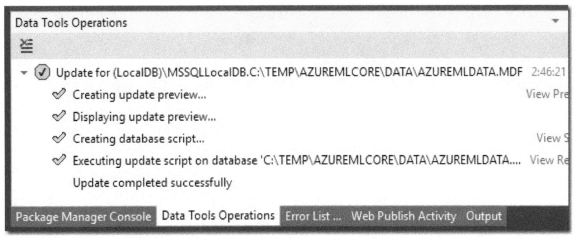

The **Data Tools Operations** window will indicate when the update is complete.

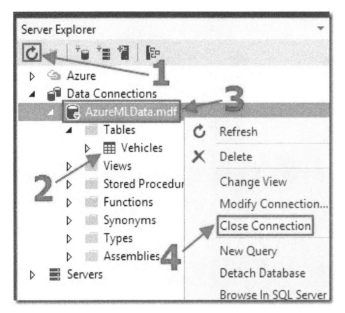

In the **Server Explorer** window, *right-click* on the database and select **Refresh**.

You will see the **Vehicles** table.

Note: Always *right-click* and select **Close Connection** to *Close* the database connection when done working with it to prevent locking.

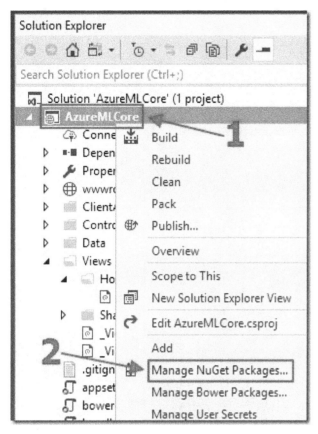

In the **Solution Explorer**, *right-click* on the project node and select **Manage NuGet Packages**.

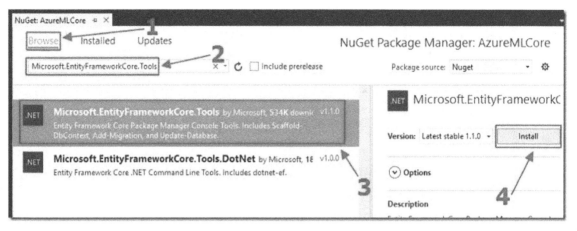

Search for and install: **Microsoft.EntityFrameworkCore.Tools**.

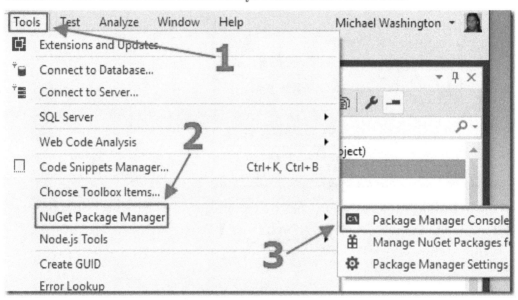

Open the **NuGet Package Manager Console**.

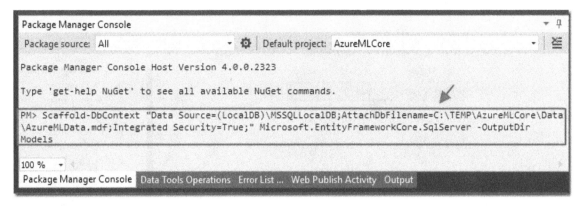

Enter:

Scaffold-DbContext "Data Source=
(LocalDB)\MSSQLLocalDB;AttachDbFilename=C:\TEMP\AzureMLCore\Data\AzureMLData.mdf;Integrated
Security=True;" Microsoft.EntityFrameworkCore.SqlServer -OutputDir Models

and press **Enter**.

(update the connection string above to point to the location of the **.mdf** file in your project).

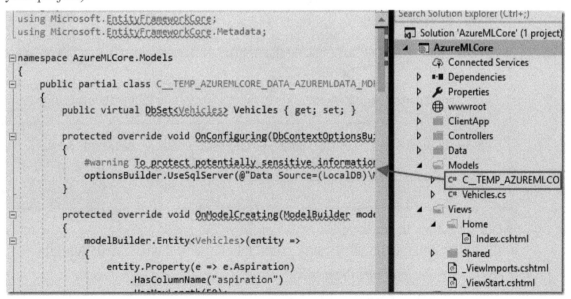

81

The *scaffolded* files will appear in the **Models** directory.

*Note: If you get **DBContext** cannot be found errors (red squiggly lines in the **Visual Studio** text editor), simply close **Visual Studio** and re-open it.*

Rename the **DataContext** file and the class to **AzureMLDataContext**.

Next, we follow the directions at this link: ASP.NET Core - Existing Database. (https://docs.microsoft.com/en-us/ef/core/get-started/aspnetcore/existing-db).

Remove the *OnConfiguring* method.

Add the following constructor to the class:

```
public AzureMLDataContext(DbContextOptions<AzureMLDataContext> options) :
base(options) { }
```

```
using Microsoft.Extensions.Configuration;
using Microsoft.Extensions.DependencyInjection;
using Microsoft.Extensions.Logging;
using AzureMLCore.Models;
using Microsoft.EntityFrameworkCore;

namespace AzureMLCore
{
    public class Startup
    {
        public Startup(IHostingEnvironment env)
        {
            var builder = new ConfigurationBuil
                .SetBasePath(env.ContentRootPat
                .AddJsonFile("appsettings.json"
                .AddJsonFile($"appsettings.{env
                .AddEnvironmentVariables();
            Configuration = builder.Build();
        }
```

Solution Explorer panel:
- wwwroot
- ClientApp
- Controllers
- Data
- Models
- Views
- .gitignore
- appsettings.json
- bower.json
- bundleconfig.json
- global.json
- package.json
- C# Program.cs
- ScaffoldingReadMe.txt
- Startup.cs
- tsconfig.json
- web.config

Add the following **using** statements to **Startup.cs**:

```
using AzureMLCore.Models;
using Microsoft.EntityFrameworkCore;
```

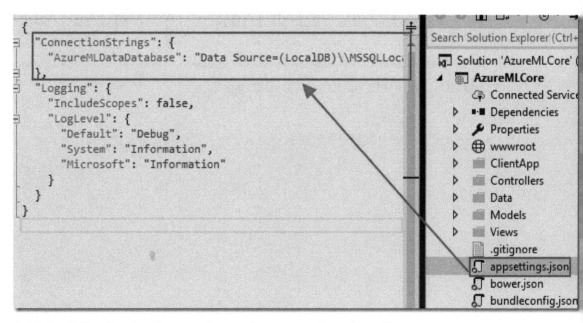

Add the following code to the **ConfigureServices** section to configure the database setting:

```
services.AddDbContext<AzureMLDataContext>(
    options => options.UseSqlServer(
        Configuration.GetConnectionString("AzureMLDataDatabase")));
```

Add the following database setting to the **appsettings.json** file:

```
"ConnectionStrings": {
  "AzureMLDataDatabase": "Data Source=(LocalDB)\\MSSQLLocalDB;AttachDbFilename=
  C:\\Temp\\AzureMLCore\\Data\\AzureMLData.mdf;Integrated Security=True;"
},
```

(Note: The *AzureMLDataDatabase* value needs to be on a single line – see the source code on AiHelpWebsite.com for the exact setting).

Create Code To Call Azure Machine Learning Web Service

We will now create the code that will call the **Azure Machine Learning** web service (that was created in **Chapter Two**), passing the parameters (such as *make*, *horsepower*, and *body style*) and retrieve a response from the web service in the form of a *predicted price*.

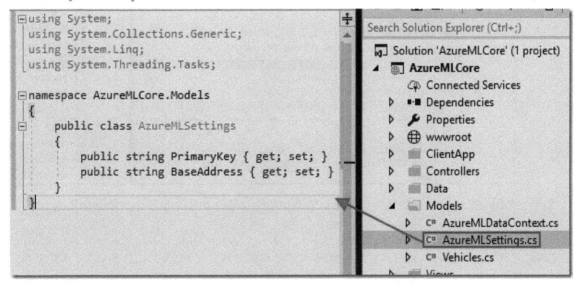

First, we need to create a class that will pass the settings (*PrimaryKey* and *BaseAddress*) from the *app settings* file to the code we will create.

Create a file called **AzureMLSettings.cs** using the following code:

```
using System;
using System.Collections.Generic;
using System.Linq;
using System.Threading.Tasks;
namespace AzureMLCore.Models
{
    public class AzureMLSettings
    {
        public string PrimaryKey { get; set; }
        public string BaseAddress { get; set; }
    }
}
```

```
10    // This method gets called by the runtime. Use this me
11    public void ConfigureServices(IServiceCollection servi
12    {
13        // Add framework services.
14        services.AddMvc();
15        services.AddDbContext<AzureMLDataContext>(
16            options => options.UseSqlServer(
17                Configuration.GetConnectionString("AzureML
18        // Get the AzureMLSettings
19        services.Configure<AzureMLSettings>(
20            Configuration.GetSection("AzureMLSettings"));
21    }
22
23    // This method gets called by the runtime. Use this me
24    public void Configure(IApplicationBuilder app, IHostin
25    {
```

```
                    ▷   C# Vehicles.cs
                    ▷   ▦ Views
                        ▤ .gitignore
                        ⬙ appsettings.json
                        ⬙ bower.json
                        ⬙ bundleconfig.json
                        ⬙ global.json
                        ⬙ package.json
                    ▷   C# Program.cs
                        ▤ ScaffoldingReadMe.txt
                    ▷   C# Startup.cs
                        ⬙ tsconfig.json
                        ▱ web.config
                    ▷   ⬙ webpack.config.js
```

Add the following code to the *ConfigureServices* method in the **Startup.cs** file:

```
// Get the AzureMLSettings
        services.Configure<AzureMLSettings>(
            Configuration.GetSection("AzureMLSettings"));
```

86

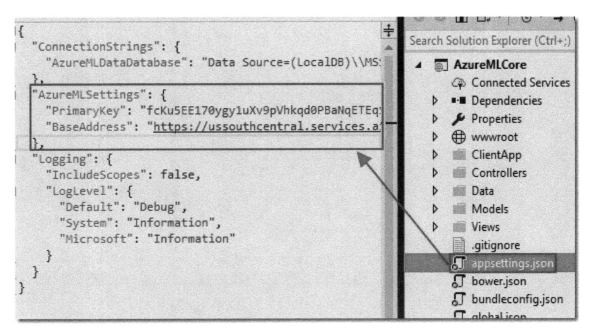

Next, add the settings to the **appsettings.json** file, replacing {{ **API Key** }} and {{ **Base Address** }} with the values you saved earlier:

```
"AzureMLSettings": {
  "PrimaryKey": "{{ API Key }}",
  "BaseAddress": "{{ Base Address }}"
},
```

The values will be retrieved and passed to the web service using code we will create in the following steps.

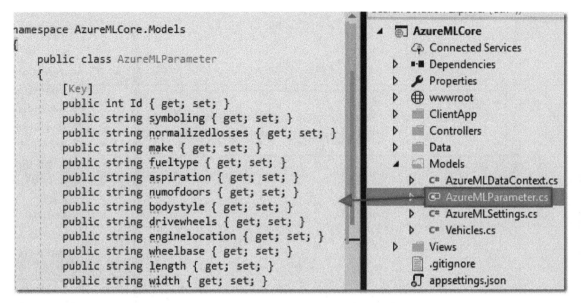

Create a file called **AzureMLParameter.cs** using the following code:

```csharp
using System.ComponentModel.DataAnnotations;
namespace AzureMLCore.Models
{
    public class AzureMLParameter
    {
        [Key]
        public int Id { get; set; }
        public string symboling { get; set; }
        public string normalizedlosses { get; set; }
        public string make { get; set; }
        public string fueltype { get; set; }
        public string aspiration { get; set; }
        public string numofdoors { get; set; }
        public string bodystyle { get; set; }
        public string drivewheels { get; set; }
        public string enginelocation { get; set; }
        public string wheelbase { get; set; }
        public string length { get; set; }
        public string width { get; set; }
        public string height { get; set; }
        public string curbweight { get; set; }
        public string enginetype { get; set; }
        public string numofcylinders { get; set; }
        public string enginesize { get; set; }
        public string fuelsystem { get; set; }
        public string bore { get; set; }
        public string stroke { get; set; }
        public string compressionratio { get; set; }
        public string horsepower { get; set; }
        public string peakrpm { get; set; }
        public string citympg { get; set; }
        public string highwaympg { get; set; }
        public string price { get; set; }
        public string Scoredlabels { get; set; }
    }
}
```

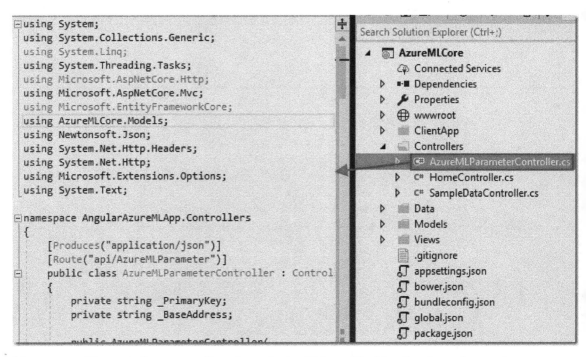

Next, we will create the *controller* class, that will be called by the **Angular** code, that will call the web service.

Create a file called **AzureMLParameterController.cs** using the following code:

```csharp
using System;
using System.Collections.Generic;
using System.Linq;
using System.Threading.Tasks;
using Microsoft.AspNetCore.Http;
using Microsoft.AspNetCore.Mvc;
using Microsoft.EntityFrameworkCore;
using AzureMLCore.Models;
using Newtonsoft.Json;
using System.Net.Http.Headers;
using System.Net.Http;
using Microsoft.Extensions.Options;
using System.Text;
namespace AngularAzureMLApp.Controllers
{
    [Produces("application/json")]
    [Route("api/AzureMLParameter")]
    public class AzureMLParameterController : Controller
    {
        // Global values to hold the PrimaryKey and BaseAddress
        private string _PrimaryKey;
        private string _BaseAddress;
        // This is the default contructor for the class
        // We will inject the AzureMLSettings when the class
        // is instantiated
        public AzureMLParameterController(
            IOptions<AzureMLSettings> AzureMLSettings)
        {
            // Set the values for PrimaryKey and BaseAddress
            _PrimaryKey = AzureMLSettings.Value.PrimaryKey;
            _BaseAddress = AzureMLSettings.Value.BaseAddress;
        }
        #region public IHttpActionResult Post(AzureMLParameter paramAzureMLParameter)
        // POST: odata/AzureMLParameter
        [HttpPost]
        public async Task<IActionResult> Post([FromBody] AzureMLParameter paramAzureMLParameter)
        {
            // Call the web service
            string ScoredLabels = await InvokeRequestResponseService(paramAzureMLParameter);
            paramAzureMLParameter.Scoredlabels = ScoredLabels;
            // Return the result
            return Ok(paramAzureMLParameter);
        }
        #endregion
```

Azure Machine Learning Studio for The Non-Data Scientist

```
// Helpers
#region async Task<string> InvokeRequestResponseService(AzureMLParameter objAzureMLParameter)
async Task<string> InvokeRequestResponseService(AzureMLParameter objAzureMLParameter)
{
    string strResponse = "";
    try
    {
        // Get the Global values for PrimaryKey and BaseAddress
        string PrimaryKey = _PrimaryKey;
        string BaseAddress = _BaseAddress;
        using (var client = new HttpClient())
        {
            // We will create a request to the web service
            // Note: The only columns that are actually being used by the Model and that need to be set:

            // highwaympg, citympg, horsepower, fuelsystem, enginesize, numofcylinders
            // enginetype, bodystyle, make, curbweight, wheelbase, numofdoors, fueltype

            var scoreRequest = new
            {
                Inputs = new Dictionary<string, StringTable>() {
                    {
                        "input1",
                        new StringTable()
                        {
                            ColumnNames = new string[] {
                                "symboling", "normalized-losses","make","fuel-type","aspiration",
                                "num-of-doors","body-style","drive-wheels","engine-location",
                                "wheel-base","length","width", "height","curb-weight","engine-type",
                                "num-of-cylinders","engine-size","fuel-system","bore","stroke",
                                "compression-ratio","horsepower","peak-rpm","city-mpg","highway-mpg","price")
```

```csharp
                    Values = new string[,] {
                        {
                            objAzureMLParameter.symboling,
                            objAzureMLParameter.normalizedlosses,
                            objAzureMLParameter.make,
                            objAzureMLParameter.fueltype,
                            objAzureMLParameter.aspiration,
                            objAzureMLParameter.numofdoors,
                            objAzureMLParameter.bodystyle,
                            objAzureMLParameter.drivewheels,
                            objAzureMLParameter.enginelocation,
                            objAzureMLParameter.wheelbase,
                            objAzureMLParameter.length,
                            objAzureMLParameter.width,
                            objAzureMLParameter.height,
                            objAzureMLParameter.curbweight,
                            objAzureMLParameter.enginetype,
                            objAzureMLParameter.numofcylinders,
                            objAzureMLParameter.enginesize,
                            objAzureMLParameter.fuelsystem,
                            objAzureMLParameter.bore,
                            objAzureMLParameter.stroke,
                            objAzureMLParameter.compressionratio,
                            objAzureMLParameter.horsepower,
                            objAzureMLParameter.peakrpm,
                            objAzureMLParameter.citympg,
                            objAzureMLParameter.highwaympg,
                            objAzureMLParameter.price
                        }
                    }
                }
            },
        },
            GlobalParameters = new Dictionary<string, string>()
            {
            }
        };
        // Create an authorization value
        client.DefaultRequestHeaders.Authorization =
            new AuthenticationHeaderValue("Bearer", PrimaryKey);
        // Call the web service
        HttpResponseMessage response =
            await client.PostAsync(new Uri(BaseAddress),
            new StringContent(JsonConvert.SerializeObject(scoreRequest),
            Encoding.UTF8, "application/json"));
```

```
            if (response.IsSuccessStatusCode)
            {
                // The call was a success -- get the response
                string result = await response.Content.ReadAsStringAsync().ConfigureAwait(false);
                Rootobject obj = JsonConvert.DeserializeObject<Rootobject>(result);
                // The predicted price is in the last element
                int intLastElement = (obj.Results.output1.value.Values[0].Count() - 1);
                var Price = obj.Results.output1.value.Values[0][intLastElement];
                // Convert the value to a currency string
                strResponse = Convert.ToDecimal(Price).ToString("C");
            }
            else
            {
                // The call returned an error
                var strContent = await response.Content.ReadAsStringAsync();
                strResponse = string.Format("The request failed with status code: {0}",
                    response.StatusCode);
                // Add the headers - they include the request ID and the timestamp,
                // which are useful for debugging the failure
                strResponse = strResponse + " " + response.Headers.ToString();
                strResponse = strResponse + " " + strContent;
            }
        }
    }
    catch (Exception ex)
    {
        return ex.Message;
    }
    return strResponse;
}
#endregion
```

```
#region public class StringTable
public class StringTable
{
    public string[] ColumnNames { get; set; }
    public string[,] Values { get; set; }
}
#endregion
#region JSON Result Classes
public class Rootobject
{
    public Results Results { get; set; }
}
public class Results
{
    public Output1 output1 { get; set; }
}
public class Output1
{
    public string type { get; set; }
    public Value value { get; set; }
}
public class Value
{
    public string[] ColumnNames { get; set; }
    public string[] ColumnTypes { get; set; }
    public string[][] Values { get; set; }
}
#endregion
    }
}
```

Create The Angular Application

We will now build the **Angular** part of the application.

Highlight all the files under: *…\ClientApp\app*

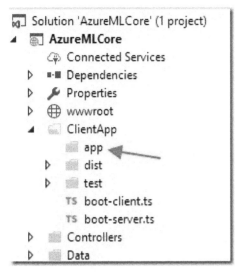

...and **delete** them.

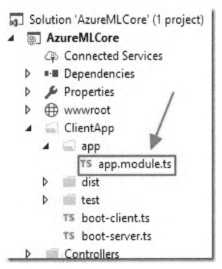

The entry point for the custom code for the application is in **app.module.ts**.

Create the file using the following code:

```typescript
import { NgModule } from '@angular/core';
import { RouterModule } from '@angular/router';
import { UniversalModule } from 'angular2-universal';
import { AppComponent } from './app.component'
import { BrowserModule } from '@angular/platform-browser';
import { HttpModule } from '@angular/http';
import { FormsModule } from '@angular/forms';
import {
    InputTextModule,
    DropdownModule,
    ButtonModule,
    FieldsetModule,
    TreeModule,
    TreeNode,
    SelectItem,
    TabMenuModule,
    MenuItem,
    TabViewModule,
    PanelModule,
    InputSwitchModule,
    PasswordModule
} from 'primeng/primeng';
import { PriceVehicleComponent } from './priceVehicle/priceVehicle.component';
import { PriceVehicleService } from './priceVehicle/priceVehicle.service';
@NgModule({
    bootstrap: [ AppComponent ],
    declarations: [
        AppComponent,
        PriceVehicleComponent,
    ],
    imports: [
        UniversalModule, // Must be first import.
        BrowserModule,
        HttpModule,
        FormsModule,
        InputTextModule,
        TreeModule,
        DropdownModule,
        ButtonModule,
        FieldsetModule,
        TabMenuModule,
        TabViewModule,
        PanelModule,
        InputSwitchModule,
        PasswordModule
    ],
    providers: [
        PriceVehicleService
    ]
})
export class AppModule {
}
```

*(**Note:** you will see red squiggly lines in the Visual Studio editor because there are files being referenced that we have not created yet.)*

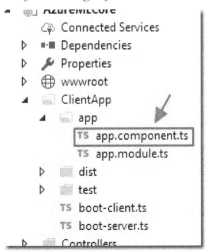

app.module, in its *bootstrap* setting, indicates that **AppComponent** is the first *component* to be loaded.

To implement it, create the file: **app.component.ts** using the following code:

```
import { Component } from '@angular/core';
@Component({
    selector: 'app',
    templateUrl: './app.component.html',
    styleUrls: ['./app.component.css']
})
export class AppComponent {
}
```

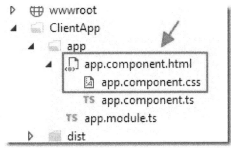

app.component.ts specifies **app.component.html** for *templateUrl* and **app.component.css** for *styleUrls*.

Create those files and implement them using the following code:

app.component.html:

```
<priceVehicle-form>Loading...</priceVehicle-form>
```

app.component.css:

```
@media (max-width: 767px) {
    /* On small screens, the nav menu spans the full width of the screen.
    Leave a space for it. */
    .body-content {
        padding-top: 50px;
    }
}
```

```
▷  ⊕ wwwroot
▲  🗀 ClientApp
    ▲  🗀 app
➤        🗀 priceVehicle
        ▷  🗋 app.component.html
           TS app.module.ts
    ▷  🗀 dist
```

The primary code for the application will be placed in the **priceVehicle** folder.

Create It.

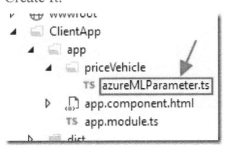

We will create an *interface* that will allow us to communicate with the **AzureMLParameterController.cs** file using a strongly typed class.

99

Azure Machine Learning Studio for The Non-Data Scientist

Create a file: **azureMLParameter.ts** using the following code:

```typescript
/* Defines the AzureMLParameter entity */
export interface IAzureMLParameter {
    id: number;
    symboling: string;
    normalizedlosses: string;
    make: string;
    fueltype: string;
    aspiration: string;
    numofdoors: string;
    bodystyle: string;
    drivewheels: string;
    enginelocation: string;
    wheelbase: string;
    length: string;
    width: string;
    height: string;
    curbweight: string;
    enginetype: string;
    numofcylinders: string;
    enginesize: string;
    fuelsystem: string;
    bore: string;
    stroke: string;
    compressionratio: string;
    horsepower: string;
    peakrpm: string;
    citympg: string;
    highwaympg: string;
    price: string; // price we submit
    scoredlabels: string; // prediction we get back
}
```

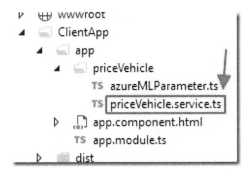

We will create a *service* that will communicate with the **C#** controller code, both to get **price predictions** and to save **actual prices** to the database.

Create a file: **priceVehicle.service.ts** using the following code:

```
import { Injectable } from '@angular/core';
import { Http, Response, RequestOptions, Request, RequestMethod, Headers } from '@angular/http';
import { Observable } from 'rxjs/Observable';
import 'rxjs/add/operator/do';
import 'rxjs/add/operator/catch';
import 'rxjs/add/operator/map';
import { IAzureMLParameter } from './azureMLParameter';
@Injectable()
export class PriceVehicleService {
    constructor(private _http: Http) { }
    priceVehicle(AzureMLParameter: IAzureMLParameter): Observable<IAzureMLParameter> {
        var _Url = 'api/AzureMLParameter';
        AzureMLParameter.price = "0";
        // This is a Post so we have to pass Headers
        let headers = new Headers({ 'Content-Type': 'application/json' });
        let options = new RequestOptions({ headers: headers });
        // Make the Angular 2 Post
        // passing the AzureMLParameter
        return this._http.post(_Url, JSON.stringify(AzureMLParameter), options)
            .map((response: Response) => <IAzureMLParameter>response.json())
            .catch(this.handleError);
    }
    recordPrice(AzureMLParameter: IAzureMLParameter): Observable<IAzureMLParameter> {
        var _Url = 'api/Vehicles';
        // This is a Post so we have to pass Headers
        let headers = new Headers({ 'Content-Type': 'application/json' });
        let options = new RequestOptions({ headers: headers });
        // Make the Angular 2 Post
        // passing the AzureMLParameter
        return this._http.post(_Url, JSON.stringify(AzureMLParameter), options)
            .map((response: Response) => <IAzureMLParameter>response.json())
            .catch(this.handleError);
    }
    // Utility
    private handleError(error: Response) {
        // in a real world app, we may send the server to some remote logging infrastructure
        // instead of just logging it to the console
        console.error(error);
        return Observable.throw(error.json().error || 'Server error');
    }
}
```

(Note: *we have implemented code to save recorded prices, but we have not added the server-side C# code yet.)*

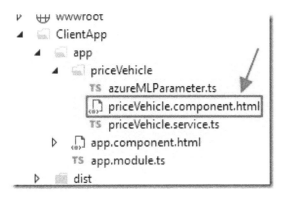

Next, we will add the actual markup for the application.

Create a file: **priceVehicle.component.html** using the following code:

```
<div style="width:800px">
    <br /><br /><br />
    <div>
        <span style="background-color: #FFFF00">{{errorMessage}}</span>
    </div>
    <h3 class="first">Price A Vehicle</h3>
    <button pButton type="button" label="Export Data" (click)="getVehicles()" class="ui-button-secondary"></but
ton>
    <div class="ui-grid ui-grid-responsive ui-grid-pad">
        <div class="ui-grid-row">
            <div class="ui-grid-col-6">
                <div class="ui-grid-col-4">
                    Make:
                </div>
                <div class="ui-grid-col-8">
                    <p-dropdown id="Make"
                                [options]="makeDropdown"
                                [(ngModel)]="AzureMLParameter.make"
                                [style]="{'width':'150px'}"></p-dropdown>
                </div>
            </div>
            <div class="ui-grid-col-6">
                <div class="ui-grid-col-4">
                    Fuel type:
                </div>
                <div class="ui-grid-col-8">
                    <p-dropdown id="FuelType"
                                [options]="fueltypeDropdown"
                                [(ngModel)]="AzureMLParameter.fueltype"
                                [style]="{'width':'150px'}"></p-dropdown>
                </div>
            </div>
        </div>
        <div class="ui-grid-row">
            <div class="ui-grid-col-6">
                <div class="ui-grid-col-4">
                    Num of doors:
                </div>
                <div class="ui-grid-col-8">
                    <p-dropdown id="NumOfDoors"
                                [options]="numofdoorsDropdown"
                                [(ngModel)]="AzureMLParameter.numofdoors"
                                [style]="{'width':'150px'}"></p-dropdown>
                </div>
            </div>
```

```
<div class="ui-grid-row">
    <div class="ui-grid-col-6">
        <div class="ui-grid-col-4">
            Wheel base:
        </div>
        <div class="ui-grid-col-8">
            <input type="text" id="WheelBase" pInputText [(ngModel)]="AzureMLParameter.wheelbase" />
        </div>
    </div>
    <div class="ui-grid-col-6">
        <div class="ui-grid-col-4">
            Curb weight:
        </div>
        <div class="ui-grid-col-8">
            <input type="text" id="CurbWeight" pInputText [(ngModel)]="AzureMLParameter.curbweight" />
        </div>
    </div>
</div>
<div class="ui-grid-row">
    <div class="ui-grid-col-6">
        <div class="ui-grid-col-4">
            Engine type:
        </div>
        <div class="ui-grid-col-8">
            <p-dropdown id="EngineType"
                        [options]="enginetypeDropdown"
                        [(ngModel)]="AzureMLParameter.enginetype"
                        [style]="{'width':'150px'}"></p-dropdown>
        </div>
    </div>
    <div class="ui-grid-col-6">
        <div class="ui-grid-col-4">
            Num of cylinders:
        </div>
        <div class="ui-grid-col-8">
            <p-dropdown id="NumOfCylinders"
                        [options]="numofcylindersDropdown"
                        [(ngModel)]="AzureMLParameter.numofcylinders"
                        [style]="{'width':'150px'}"></p-dropdown>
        </div>
    </div>
</div>
```

```
<div class="ui-grid-row">
    <div class="ui-grid-col-6">
        <div class="ui-grid-col-4">
            Engine size:
        </div>
        <div class="ui-grid-col-8">
            <input type="text" id="EngineSize" pInputText [(ngModel)]="AzureMLParameter.enginesize" />
        </div>
    </div>
    <div class="ui-grid-col-6">
        <div class="ui-grid-col-4">
            Fuel system:
        </div>
        <div class="ui-grid-col-8">
            <p-dropdown id="FuelSystem"
                        [options]="fuelsystemDropdown"
                        [(ngModel)]="AzureMLParameter.fuelsystem"
                        [style]="{'width':'150px'}"></p-dropdown>
        </div>
    </div>
</div>
<div class="ui-grid-row">
    <div class="ui-grid-col-6">
        <div class="ui-grid-col-4">
            Horsepower:
        </div>
        <div class="ui-grid-col-8">
            <input type="text" id="Horsepower" pInputText [(ngModel)]="AzureMLParameter.horsepower" />
        </div>
    </div>
    <div class="ui-grid-col-6">
        <div class="ui-grid-col-4">
            City mpg:
        </div>
        <div class="ui-grid-col-8">
            <input type="text" id="CityMpg" pInputText [(ngModel)]="AzureMLParameter.citympg" />
        </div>
    </div>
</div>
<div class="ui-grid-row">
    <div class="ui-grid-col-6">
        <div class="ui-grid-col-4">
            Highway mpg:
        </div>
        <div class="ui-grid-col-8">
            <input type="text" id="HighwayMpg" pInputText [(ngModel)]="AzureMLParameter.highwaympg" />
        </div>
    </div>
</div>
</div>
```

```
<div class="ui-grid ui-grid-responsive ui-grid-pad">
    <div class="ui-grid-row">
        <div class="ui-grid-col-6">
            <div class="ui-grid-col-4">
                <button pButton type="button" label="Price Vehicle" (click)="priceVehicle()"></button>
            </div>
            <div class="ui-grid-col-8">
                <p>Predicted Price: <b>{{AzureMLParameter.scoredlabels}}</b></p>
            </div>
        </div>
        <div class="ui-grid-col-6">
            <div class="ui-grid-col-4">
                <button pButton type="button" label="Record Price" (click)="recordPrice()"></button>
            </div>
            <div class="ui-grid-col-8">
                <input type="text" id="Price" pInputText [(ngModel)]="AzureMLParameter.price" />
            </div>
        </div>
    </div>
</div>
```

Finally, add the primary custom code for the application by creating a file called **priceVehicle.component.ts** using the following code:

```
import { Component, OnInit, OnDestroy } from '@angular/core';
import { Router, ActivatedRoute } from '@angular/router';
import { Subscription } from 'rxjs/Subscription';
import {
    SelectItem,
    InputTextModule,
    ButtonModule,
    DropdownModule
}
    from 'primeng/primeng';
import { IAzureMLParameter } from './azureMLParameter';
import { PriceVehicleService } from './priceVehicle.service';
@Component({
    selector: 'priceVehicle-form',
    templateUrl: './priceVehicle.component.html'
})
export class PriceVehicleComponent implements OnInit {
    errorMessage: string;
    AzureMLParameter: IAzureMLParameter;
    makeDropdown: SelectItem[] = [];
    fueltypeDropdown: SelectItem[] = [];
    numofdoorsDropdown: SelectItem[] = [];
    bodystyleDropdown: SelectItem[] = [];
    enginetypeDropdown: SelectItem[] = [];
    numofcylindersDropdown: SelectItem[] = [];
    fuelsystemDropdown: SelectItem[] = [];
    // Register the service
    constructor(private _PriceVehicleService: PriceVehicleService) { }
    ngOnInit(): void {
        // Set default values for vehicle parameters
        this.setDefaultValues();
        // Fill the dropdowns
        this.fillDropdowns();
    }
    priceVehicle() {
        this.errorMessage = "";
        // Get the predicted price for a vehicle
        // Call the service
        this._PriceVehicleService.priceVehicle(this.AzureMLParameter)
            .subscribe(
            AzureMLParameter => {
                this.AzureMLParameter = AzureMLParameter
            },
            error => this.errorMessage = <any>error);
    }
```

```
recordPrice() {
    this.errorMessage = "";
    // Save the price of a vehicle to the database
    // Call the service
    this._PriceVehicleService.recordPrice(this.AzureMLParameter)
        .subscribe(
        AzureMLParameter => {
            alert('Recorded: ' + AzureMLParameter.id);
        },
        error => this.errorMessage = <any>error);
}
getVehicles() {
    window.location.href = 'Home/DownloadCSV';
}
// Utility
setDefaultValues() {
    // Note: The only columns that are actually being used by the Model and that need to be set:
    // highwaympg, citympg, horsepower, fuelsystem, enginesize, numofcylinders
    // enginetype, bodystyle, make, curbweight, wheelbase, numofdoors, fueltype
    let NewAzureMLParameter: IAzureMLParameter = {
        id: 0,
        symboling: "0",
        normalizedlosses: "1",
        make: "toyota",
        fueltype: "gas",
        aspiration: " ",
        numofdoors: "four",
        bodystyle: "sedan",
        drivewheels: " ",
        enginelocation: " ",
        wheelbase: "99.4",
        length: "0",
        width: "0",
        height: "0",
        curbweight: "2824",
        enginetype: "ohc",
        numofcylinders: "five",
        enginesize: "136",
        fuelsystem: "mpfi",
        bore: "0",
        stroke: "0",
        compressionratio: "0",
        horsepower: "115",
        peakrpm: "0",
        citympg: "18",
        highwaympg: "22",
        price: "0",
        scoredlabels: " "
    }
    this.AzureMLParameter = NewAzureMLParameter;
}
```

```
fillDropdowns() {
    // makeDropdown
    this.makeDropdown.push({ label: 'toyota', value: 'toyota' });
    this.makeDropdown.push({ label: 'nissan', value: 'nissan' });
    this.makeDropdown.push({ label: 'mazda', value: 'mazda' });
    this.makeDropdown.push({ label: 'mitsubishi', value: 'mitsubishi' });
    this.makeDropdown.push({ label: 'honda', value: 'honda' });
    this.makeDropdown.push({ label: 'volkswagen', value: 'volkswagen' });
    this.makeDropdown.push({ label: 'subaru', value: 'subaru' });
    this.makeDropdown.push({ label: 'volvo', value: 'volvo' });
    this.makeDropdown.push({ label: 'peugot', value: 'peugot' });
    this.makeDropdown.push({ label: 'dodge', value: 'dodge' });
    // fueltypeDropdown
    this.fueltypeDropdown.push({ label: 'gas', value: 'gas' });
    this.fueltypeDropdown.push({ label: 'diesel', value: 'diesel' });
    // numofdoorsDropdown
    this.numofdoorsDropdown.push({ label: 'four', value: 'four' });
    this.numofdoorsDropdown.push({ label: 'two', value: 'two' });
    // bodystyleDropdown
    this.bodystyleDropdown.push({ label: 'sedan', value: 'sedan' });
    this.bodystyleDropdown.push({ label: 'hatchback', value: 'hatchback' });
    this.bodystyleDropdown.push({ label: 'wagon', value: 'wagon' });
    this.bodystyleDropdown.push({ label: 'hardtop', value: 'hardtop' });
    this.bodystyleDropdown.push({ label: 'convertible', value: 'convertible' });
    // enginetypeDropdown
    this.enginetypeDropdown.push({ label: 'ohc', value: 'ohc' });
    this.enginetypeDropdown.push({ label: 'ohcf', value: 'ohcf' });
    this.enginetypeDropdown.push({ label: 'ohcv', value: 'ohcv' });
    this.enginetypeDropdown.push({ label: 'dohc', value: 'dohc' });
    this.enginetypeDropdown.push({ label: 'l', value: 'l' });
    this.enginetypeDropdown.push({ label: 'rotor', value: 'rotor' });
    this.enginetypeDropdown.push({ label: 'dohcv', value: 'dohcv' });
    // numofcylindersDropdown
    this.numofcylindersDropdown.push({ label: 'four', value: 'four' });
    this.numofcylindersDropdown.push({ label: 'six', value: 'six' });
    this.numofcylindersDropdown.push({ label: 'five', value: 'five' });
    this.numofcylindersDropdown.push({ label: 'eight', value: 'eight' });
    this.numofcylindersDropdown.push({ label: 'two', value: 'two' });
    this.numofcylindersDropdown.push({ label: 'three', value: 'three' });
    this.numofcylindersDropdown.push({ label: 'twelve', value: 'twelve' });
    // fuelsystemDropdown
    this.fuelsystemDropdown.push({ label: 'mpfi', value: 'mpfi' });
    this.fuelsystemDropdown.push({ label: '2bbl', value: '2bbl' });
    this.fuelsystemDropdown.push({ label: 'idi', value: 'idi' });
    this.fuelsystemDropdown.push({ label: '1bbl', value: '1bbl' });
    this.fuelsystemDropdown.push({ label: 'spdi', value: 'spdi' });
    this.fuelsystemDropdown.push({ label: '4bbl', value: '4bbl' });
    this.fuelsystemDropdown.push({ label: 'mfi', value: 'mfi' });
    this.fuelsystemDropdown.push({ label: 'spfi', value: 'spfi' });
    }
}
```

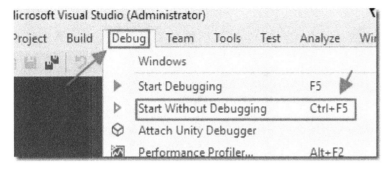

Run the application.

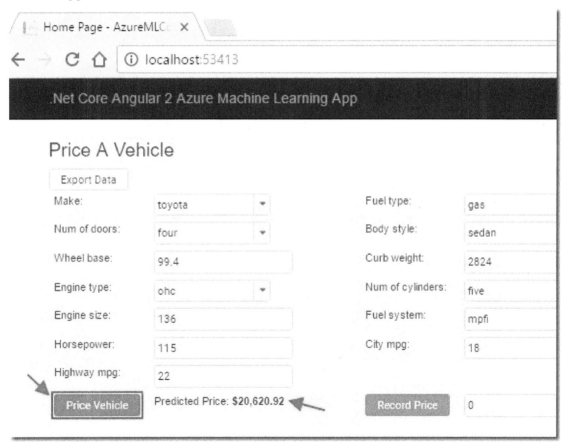

The application will show, and we can click the **Price Vehicle** button to see the *predicted price* for the options selected on the form.

Saving Data

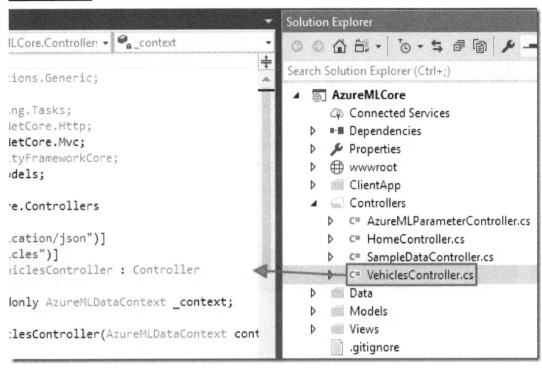

To save data, we need to add a server-side method.

Create a file at: **..\Controllers\VehiclesController.cs** using the following code:

```csharp
using System;
using System.Collections.Generic;
using System.Linq;
using System.Threading.Tasks;
using Microsoft.AspNetCore.Http;
using Microsoft.AspNetCore.Mvc;
using Microsoft.EntityFrameworkCore;
using AzureMLCore.Models;
namespace AzureMLCore.Controllers
{
    [Produces("application/json")]
    [Route("api/Vehicles")]
    public class VehiclesController : Controller
    {
        private readonly AzureMLDataContext _context;
        public VehiclesController(AzureMLDataContext context)
        {
            _context = context;
        }
        // POST: api/Vehicles
        [HttpPost]
        public IActionResult PostVehicles([FromBody] Vehicles vehicles)
        {
            if (!ModelState.IsValid)
            {
                return BadRequest(ModelState);
            }
            _context.Vehicles.Add(vehicles);
            _context.SaveChanges();
            return CreatedAtAction("GetVehicles", new { id = vehicles.Id }, vehicles);
        }
    }
}
```

Rebuild the application and re-launch or refresh it in the web browser.

We can now enter a recorded price and save it to the database.

Viewing Data

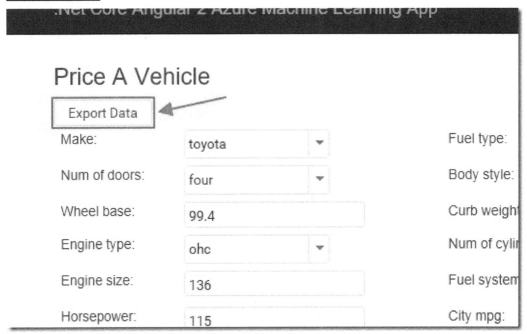

We can *export* the recorded prices.

We will use this data in the next article to retrain the **Model** used by the web service to make price predictions.

```
:Controller(Models.AzureMLDataContext contex

:t = context;


:ContentResult DownloadCSV()

ik up array so the code formats properly fo
  strArray1 = "{0},{1},{2},{3},{4},{5},{6},{
  strArray2 = "{11},{12},{13},{14},{15},{16}
  strArray3 = "{20},{21},{22},{23},{24},{25}'
  strFullArray = strArray1 + strArray2 + str/

; returns all vehicles in the database
:ult = (from vehicle in _context.Vehicles
```

- ▲ 🔲 **AzureMLCore**
  - ☁ Connected Services
  - ▷ ■-■ Dependencies
  - ▷ 🔧 Properties
  - ▷ ⊕ wwwroot
  - ▷ 🔲 ClientApp
  - ▲ 🔲 Controllers
    - ▷ C# AzureMLParameterController.cs
    - ▷ C# HomeController.cs
    - ▷ C# SampleDataController.cs
    - ▷ C# VehiclesController.cs
  - ▷ 🔲 Data
  - ▷ 🔲 Models
  - ▷ 🔲 Views

Open the **HomeController.cs** file and add the following code to the class:

115

```
private readonly Models.AzureMLDataContext _context;
       public HomeController(Models.AzureMLDataContext context)
       {
           _context = context;
       }
       public FileContentResult DownloadCSV()
       {
           // Break up array so the code formats properly for the blog post article
           string strArray1 = "{0},{1},{2},{3},{4},{5},{6},{7},{8},{9},{10},";
           string strArray2 = "{11},{12},{13},{14},{15},{16},{17},{18},{19},";
           string strArray3 = "{20},{21},{22},{23},{24},{25}\n";
           string strFullArray = strArray1 + strArray2 + strArray3;
           // This returns all vehicles in the database
           var result = (from vehicle in _context.Vehicles
                         select new Models.AzureMLParameter
                         {
                             Id = vehicle.Id,
                             symboling = vehicle.Symboling,
                             normalizedlosses = vehicle.NormalizedLosses,
                             make = vehicle.Make,
                             fueltype = vehicle.FuelType,
                             aspiration = vehicle.Aspiration,
                             numofdoors = vehicle.NumOfDoors,
                             bodystyle = vehicle.BodyStyle,
                             drivewheels = vehicle.DriveWheels,
                             enginelocation = vehicle.EngineLocation,
                             wheelbase = vehicle.WheelBase,
                             length = vehicle.Length,
                             width = vehicle.Width,
                             height = vehicle.Height,
                             curbweight = vehicle.CurbWeight,
                             enginetype = vehicle.EngineType,
                             numofcylinders = vehicle.NumOfCylinders,
                             enginesize = vehicle.EngineSize,
                             fuelsystem = vehicle.FuelSystem,
                             bore = vehicle.Bore,
                             stroke = vehicle.Stroke,
                             compressionratio = vehicle.CompressionRatio,
                             horsepower = vehicle.Horsepower,
                             peakrpm = vehicle.PeakRpm,
                             citympg = vehicle.CityMpg,
                             highwaympg = vehicle.HighwayMpg,
                             price = vehicle.Price
                         }).ToList();
```

```csharp
// Write headers
string csv = string.Format(strFullArray,
                            "symboling",
                            "normalized-losses",
                            "make",
                            "fuel-type",
                            "aspiration",
                            "num-of-doors",
                            "body-style",
                            "drive-wheels",
                            "engine-location",
                            "wheel-base",
                            "length",
                            "width",
                            "height",
                            "curb-weight",
                            "engine-type",
                            "num-of-cylinders",
                            "engine-size",
                            "fuel-system",
                            "bore",
                            "stroke",
                            "compression-ratio",
                            "horsepower",
                            "peak-rpm",
                            "city-mpg",
                            "highway-mpg",
                            "price");
```

```
// Write data
csv = csv + string.Concat(from vehicle in result
                          select string.Format(strFullArray,
                          vehicle.symboling,
                          vehicle.normalizedlosses,
                          vehicle.make,
                          vehicle.fueltype,
                          vehicle.aspiration,
                          vehicle.numofdoors,
                          vehicle.bodystyle,
                          vehicle.drivewheels,
                          vehicle.enginelocation,
                          vehicle.wheelbase,
                          vehicle.length,
                          vehicle.width,
                          vehicle.height,
                          vehicle.curbweight,
                          vehicle.enginetype,
                          vehicle.numofcylinders,
                          vehicle.enginesize,
                          vehicle.fuelsystem,
                          vehicle.bore,
                          vehicle.stroke,
                          vehicle.compressionratio,
                          vehicle.horsepower,
                          vehicle.peakrpm,
                          vehicle.citympg,
                          vehicle.highwaympg,
                          vehicle.price
                          ));
    return File(new System.Text.UTF8Encoding().GetBytes(csv), "text/csv", "vehicles.csv");
}
```

Chapter 4: Retraining an Azure Machine Learning Application

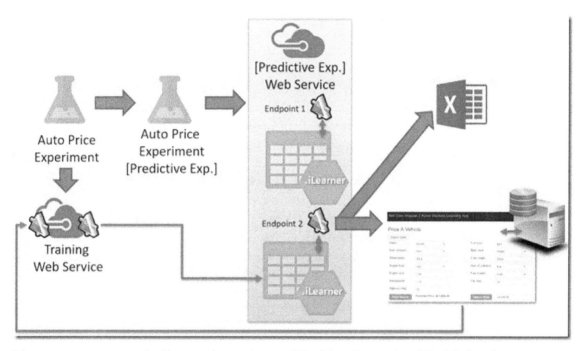

You can programmatically retrain an **Azure Machine Learning Model** thereby improving the predictions of your associated predictive applications.

In the previous chapters, we created an **Azure Machine Learning** experiment that predicts the price of a vehicle given parameters such as *make*, *horsepower*, and *body style*. It does that by creating a **Model** based on prices of previous vehicles. We then operationalized the model by creating a **web service**. Finally, we consumed that web service using an **Angular 2** application.

In this chapter, we will take the output from our **Angular 2** application (that consumes the **web service**), and update its underlying predictive **Model** by *retraining* it using new data produced by the **Angular 2** application (the **Angular 2** application allows the user to record actual prices of vehicles based on the options selected). We will then use this updated web service for future predictions.

The Retraining Process

To implement the retraining, we will perform the following steps:

- **Prepare our retraining data** - We will export recorded automobile price sales from the **Angular 2** application, and combine that data with the data we used to previously train our **Model** (each time we retrain our **Model**, we have to use all the available data).
- **Create a new *iLearner* file using the Training experiment** – We will create a new web service, using the original **Auto Price Experiment** (not the *Auto Price Experiment [Predictive Exp.]*). This will allow us to pass the new training data to it and retrieve a new *iLearner* file that we will use for future improved predictions.
- **Add a new endpoint to the Predictive Web Service and *Patch* the *iLearner* file to it** - To consume the new *iLearner* file, we will add a new web service endpoint to the **Auto Price Experiment [Predictive Exp.]** web service and perform a *Patch* to have it use the new *iLearner* **Model**. We will then point the **Angular 2** application to this new endpoint for improved predictions.

Prepare The Training Data

Currently our **Angular 2** application calls the endpoint of the **Auto Price Experiment [Predictive Exp.]** web service:

Predictive Web Service
Consumed By Angular Application

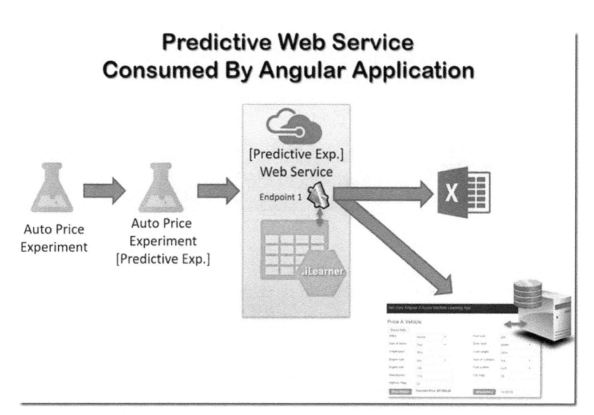

This allows us to pass parameters to the predictive **Model** and receive price predictions.

The **Angular 2** application also allows us to record prices.

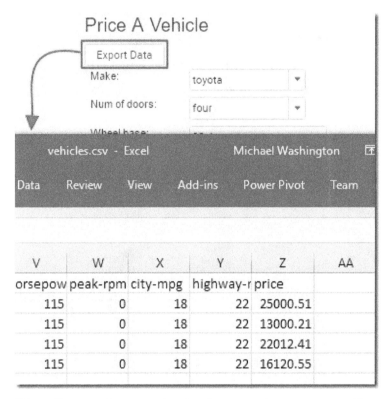

We will *record* some prices and *export* them to a **.csv** file and save it.

We will log into the Azure Machine Learning Studio and select the **Auto Price Experiment** we created earlier.

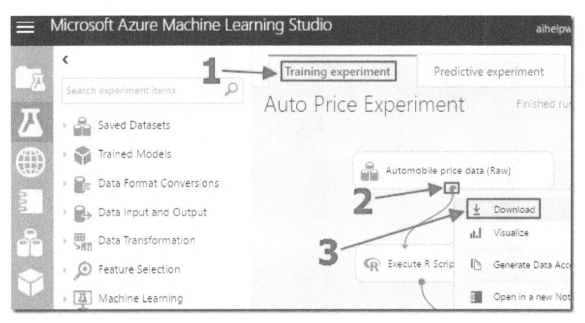

We will ensure we have selected the **Training Experiment** and we will download the **Automobile price data (Raw)** file.

200	-2	103	volvo	gas	turbo	tour	sedan	rwd	front	104.3
201	-1	74	volvo	gas	turbo	four	wagon	rwd	front	104.3
202	-1	95	volvo	gas	std	four	sedan	rwd	front	109.1
203	-1	95	volvo	gas	turbo	four	sedan	rwd	front	109.1
204	-1	95	volvo	gas	std	four	sedan	rwd	front	109.1
205	-1	95	volvo	diesel	turbo	four	sedan	rwd	front	109.1
206	-1	95	volvo	gas	turbo	four	sedan	rwd	front	109.1
207	0	1	audi	gas		four	sedan			99.4
208	0	1	volkswage	gas		four	sedan			99.4
209	0	1	audi	gas		four	sedan			99.4
210	0	1	audi	gas		four	sedan			99.4
211	0	1	audi	gas		four	sedan			99.4
212	0	1	mazda	gas		four	sedan			99.4
213	0	1	tovota	gas		four	sedan			99.4

We will cut and paste the data from the **Angular 2** application into the file and save it.

We now have our new training data.

Azure Machine Learning Studio for The Non-Data Scientist

Set-up An Azure Storage Account

We will need an Azure Storage account to perform the retraining process, so if you do not have one, go to https://portal.azure.com/ and create one by following the steps in the image above.

Next, download and install the Azure Storage Explorer from

http://storageexplorer.com/

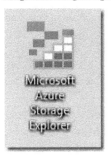

Open the **Azure Storage Explorer**.

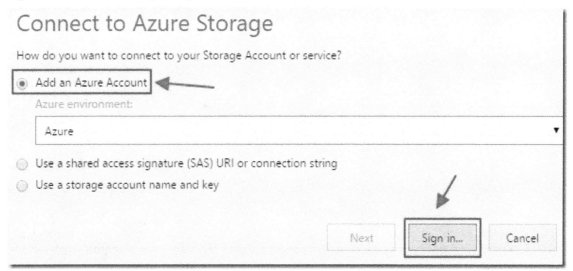

Select **Add an Azure Account** and **Sign in**.

Navigate to the **Azure storage account** you created earlier, and expand the tree to show all the nodes.

Right-click on the **Blob Containers** node and select **Create Blob Container**.

Create a container called **experimentoutput**.

We will use this container to create and store our *iLearner* **Model**.

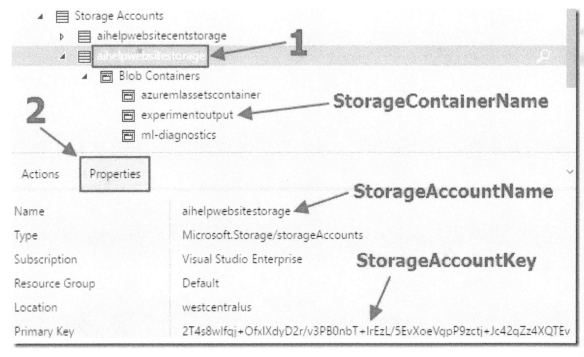

If you now click on the storage account and look in the **Properties**, you can retrieve account name and key.

Us the image above to locate and copy down the following values:

- StorageAccountName
- StorageAccountKey
- StorageContainerName

We will need these values for the **Batch Retraining** programs we will create later.

Retraining Web Service

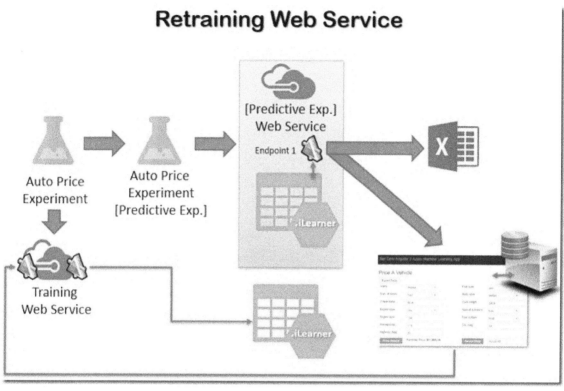

We will now create a **Retraining Web Service**.

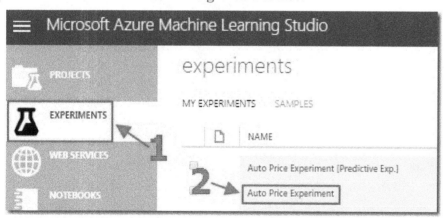

Log into the Azure Machine Learning Studio and select the **Auto Price**

Experiment we created earlier.

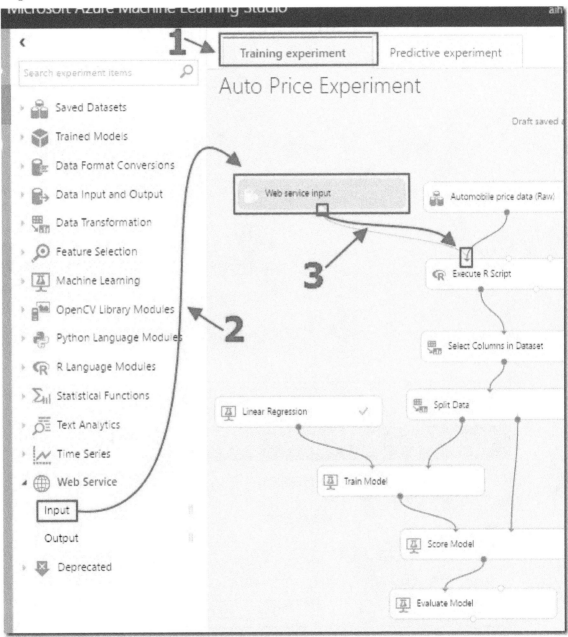

Ensure that you are on the **Training experiment** tab.

Select and drag a **Web Service** *Input* onto the design surface.

Connect it to the first input on the **Execute R Script** module.

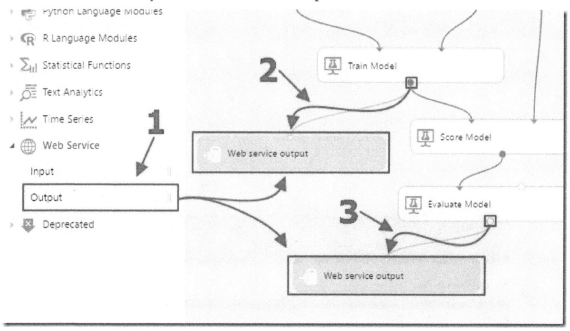

Select and drag two **Web Service** *output* modules to the design surface.

Connect one to the output of the **Train Model** module (this will be used to retrieve the *iLearner* file into the **Azure Storage** container).

Connect one to the output of the **Evaluate Model** module (this will be used to retrieve a **.csv** file into the **Azure Storage** container, which will indicate how well the **Model** currently performs).

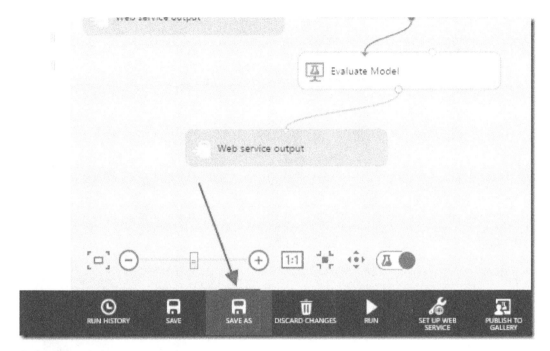

Select **Save As**.

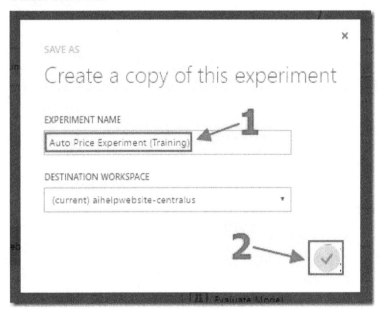

Name the experiment **Auto Price Experiment (Training)**.

Note: At this time, retraining works best in workspaces in the Central US Azure region.

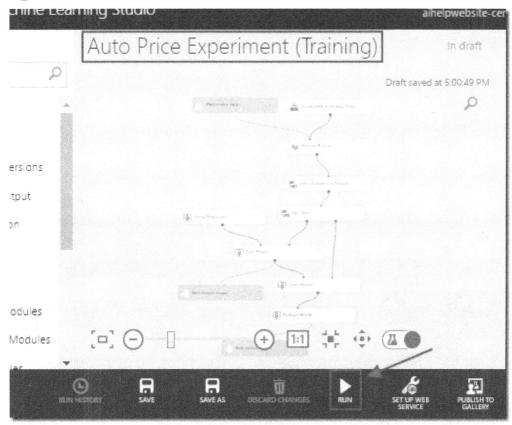

You will now be in the new experiment.

Click the **Run** button (to validate the experiment).

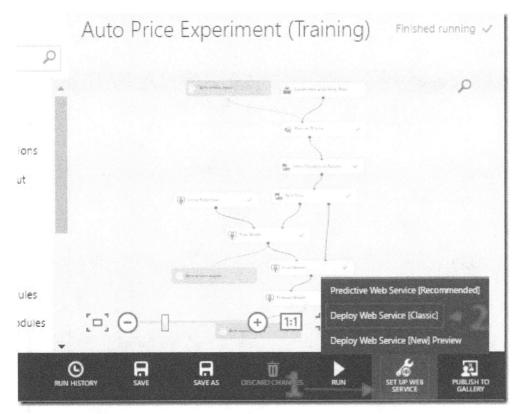

Next, click the **Set Up Web Service** button and select **Deploy Web Service (Classic)**.

If we switch to the **Web Services** node we can see the newly created **Auto Price Experiment (Training)** web service.

Click on it to select it.

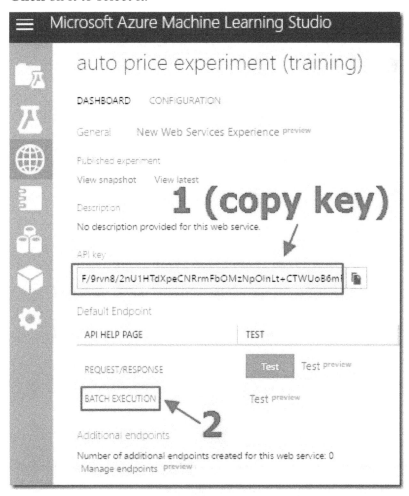

This will take you to the **Dashboard** for the **Web Service**.

Copy the **API key** and save it. You will need this for the **Batch Retraining** program we will create later.

When we submit data to retrain the web service, it must be done as a *Batch Execution*.

Click the **Batch Execution** link.

Azure Machine Learning Studio for The Non-Data Scientist

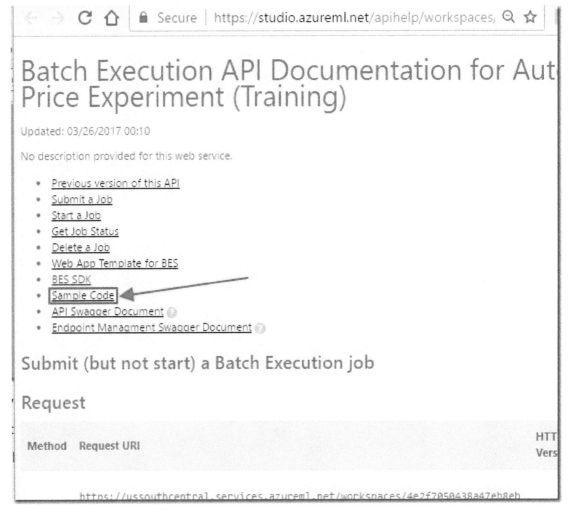

This will open the configuration page for the web service.

Click the **Sample Code** button.

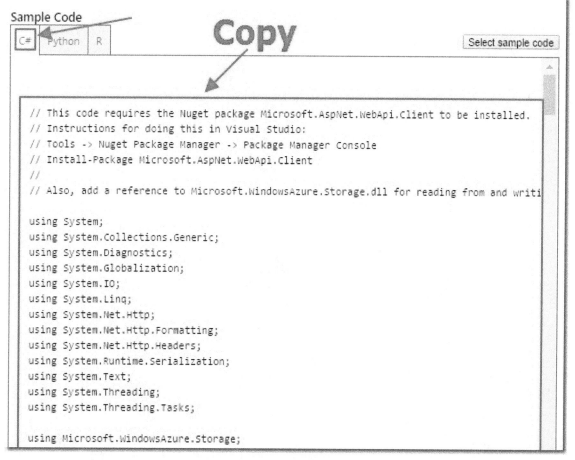

Sample Code

Copy

Select sample code

```
// This code requires the Nuget package Microsoft.AspNet.WebApi.Client to be installed.
// Instructions for doing this in Visual Studio:
// Tools -> Nuget Package Manager -> Package Manager Console
// Install-Package Microsoft.AspNet.WebApi.Client
//
// Also, add a reference to Microsoft.WindowsAzure.Storage.dll for reading from and writi

using System;
using System.Collections.Generic;
using System.Diagnostics;
using System.Globalization;
using System.IO;
using System.Linq;
using System.Net.Http;
using System.Net.Http.Formatting;
using System.Net.Http.Headers;
using System.Runtime.Serialization;
using System.Text;
using System.Threading;
using System.Threading.Tasks;

using Microsoft.WindowsAzure.Storage;
```

This will take you to the sample code to call the web service.

Click on the **C#** tab and *copy* all the code.

Create The Batch Retraining Program

Open **Visual Studio 2017**.

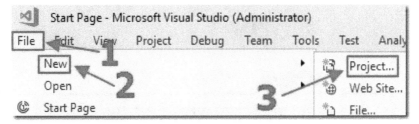

Select **File** then **New** then **Project**.

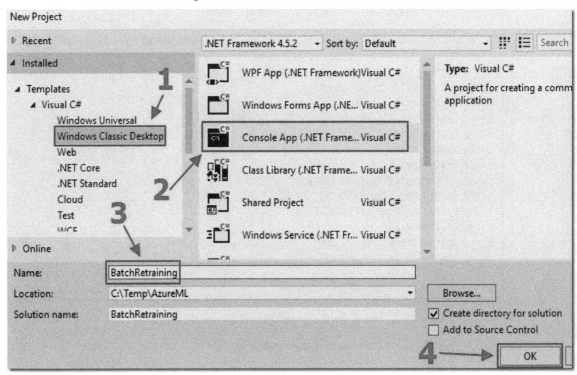

Create a new **Console App**.

```
using System.IO;
using System.Linq;
using System.Net.Http;
using System.Net.Http.Formatting;
using System.Net.Http.Headers;
using System.Runtime.Serialization;
using System.Text;
using System.Threading;
using System.Threading.Tasks;

using Microsoft.WindowsAzure.Storage;
using Microsoft.WindowsAzure.Storage.Auth;
using Microsoft.WindowsAzure.Storage.Blob;

namespace CallBatchExecutionService
{
    public class AzureBlobDataReference
    {
        // Storage connection string used for regular blobs. I
        // DefaultEndpointsProtocol=https;AccountName=ACCOUNT
        // It's not used for shared access signature blobs.
        public string ConnectionString { get; set; }
```

Search Solution Explorer (Ctrl+

- Solution 'BatchRetraining
  - C# **BatchRetraining**
    - ▷ 🔧 Properties
    - ▷ ▪▪ References
    - 🗗 App.config
    - ▷ C# Program.cs

Open the **Program.cs** file and replace *all* the code with the code you copied from the **Azure Machine Learning Studio** web site.

```
2
3    // This code requires the Nuget package Microsoft.AspNet.WebApi.Client to be installed.
4    // Instructions for doing this in Visual Studio:
5    // Tools -> Nuget Package Manager -> Package Manager Console
6    // Install-Package Microsoft.AspNet.WebApi.Client
7    //
8    // Also, add a reference to Microsoft.WindowsAzure.Storage.dll for
9    // reading from and writing to the Azure blob storage
10
```

Follow the directions, at the top of the code, to install the required assemblies:

- Install-Package Microsoft.AspNet.WebApi.Client
- Install-Package WindowsAzure.Storage

```
145    // 3. Call the Batch Execution Service to process the data in the
146    // 4. Download the output blob, if any, to local file
147
148    const string BaseUrl = "https://ussouthcentral.services.azureml.ne
149
150    const string StorageAccountName = "aihelpwebsitestorage"; // Repla
151    const string StorageAccountKey = "2T4s8wIfqj+OfxlXdyD2r/v3PB0nbT+l
152    const string StorageContainerName = "experimentoutput"; // Replace
153    string storageConnectionString = string.Format("DefaultEndpointsPr
154    const string apiKey = "F/9rvn8/2nU1HTdXpeCNRrmFbOMzNpOlnLt+CTWUoB6
155
156    // set a time out for polling status
157    const int TimeOutInMilliseconds = 120 * 1000; // Set a timeout of
158
159
160
161    UploadFileToBlob(@"C:\TEMP\AzureML\AutomobilepricedataRaw.csv" /*R
162        "input1datablob.csv" /*Replace this with the name you would lik
163        StorageContainerName, storageConnectionString);
164
165    using (HttpClient client = new HttpClient())
166    {
167        var request = new BatchExecutionRequest()
168        {
169
```

Update the code with the values saved from the earlier steps.

Set the value for **UploadFileToBlob** to the location on your computer where you saved the **.csv** file we downloaded earlier (and updated with the data from the **Angular 2** application).

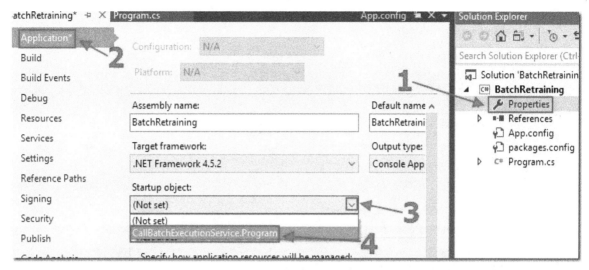

Select **Properties** in the **Solution Explorer**, then **Application**, then **Startup object**, and select the **CallBatchExecutionService.Program** method.

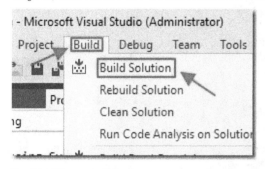

Build The application

```
var container = BlobClient.GetContainerReference(storage
    container.CreateIfNotExists();
    var blob = container.GetBlockBlobReference(inputBlobName
    blob.UploadFromFile(inputFileLocation, FileMode.Open);
}
```

Note: If you get the error:

Argument 2: cannot convert from 'System.IO.FileMode' to 'Microsoft.WindowsAzure.Storage.AccessCondition'

Simply remove the **FileMode.Open** value.

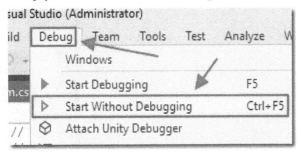

Run the application.

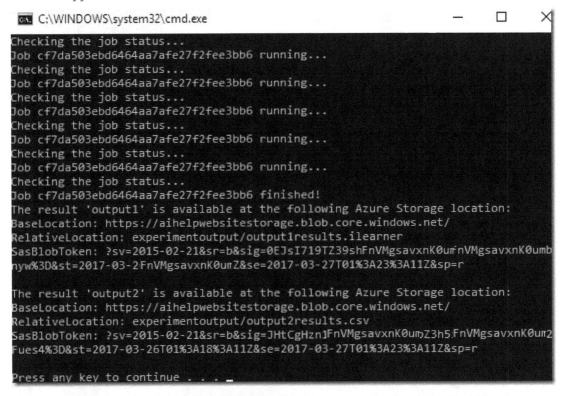

The job will run and inform you when it is finished.

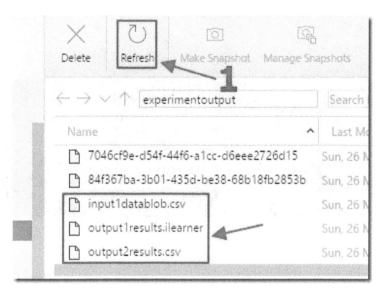

If we open the container in the **Azure Storage Explorer**, we will see the input file (that was uploaded by the program we created), and the output files.

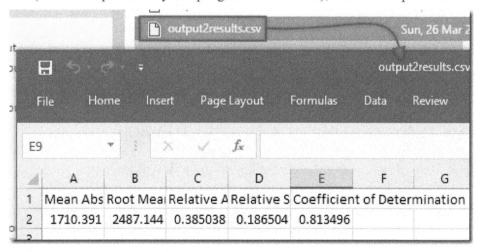

For example, we can open the output **.csv** file to see the output from the **Evaluate Model** module.

*Note: See Evaluate Model (*https://msdn.microsoft.com/en-us/library/azure/dn905915.aspx*) for instructions on how to properly interpret results. For example, with Coefficient of Determination, "...caution should be* *used in interpreting R2 values, as low values can be entirely normal and high values can be suspect."*

Get Required Values

```
Job cf7da503ebd6464aa7afe27f2fee3bb6 finished!
The result 'output1' is available at the following Azure Storage location:
BaseLocation: https://aihelpwebsitestorage.blob.core.windows.net/
RelativeLocation: experimentoutput/output1results.ilearner
SasBlobToken: ?sv=2015-02-21&sr=b&sig=0EJsI719TZ39shFnVMgsavxnK0urnVMgsavxnK0u
nyw%3D&st=2017-03-2FnVMgsavxnK0urZ&se=2017-03-27T01%3A23%3A11Z&sp=r

The result 'output2' is available at the following Azure Storage location:
BaseLocation: https://aihelpwebsitestorage.blob.core.windows.net/
```

The output will contain following values that you will need for the final step:

- BaseLocation
- RelativeLocation
- SasBlobToken

You will want to gather the values for the output that creates the *iLearner* file (<u>not</u> the output that creates the **.csv** file).

This is how you would get the values for a normal *automated* process.

Note: The **SasBlobToken** represents a *lease* for a Shared Access Signature (https://docs.microsoft.com/en-us/rest/api/storageservices/fileservices/delegating-access-with-a-shared-access-signature) to the *iLearner* file that will expire in *1.5* hours. If you don't complete the final step (*patching* a new endpoint on the predictive web service by updating it with the new *iLearner* file) the *lease* will *expire*. The file will remain but the access key to get to it will no longer work. You can obtain a new key by running the previous process again, or by using the **Azure Storage Explorer**.

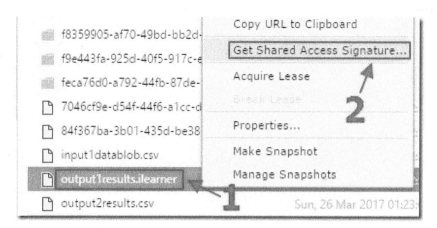

If you do need to get a new access key, open the **Azure Storage Explorer**, locate the *iLearner* file, *right-click* on it, and select **Get Shared Access Signature**.

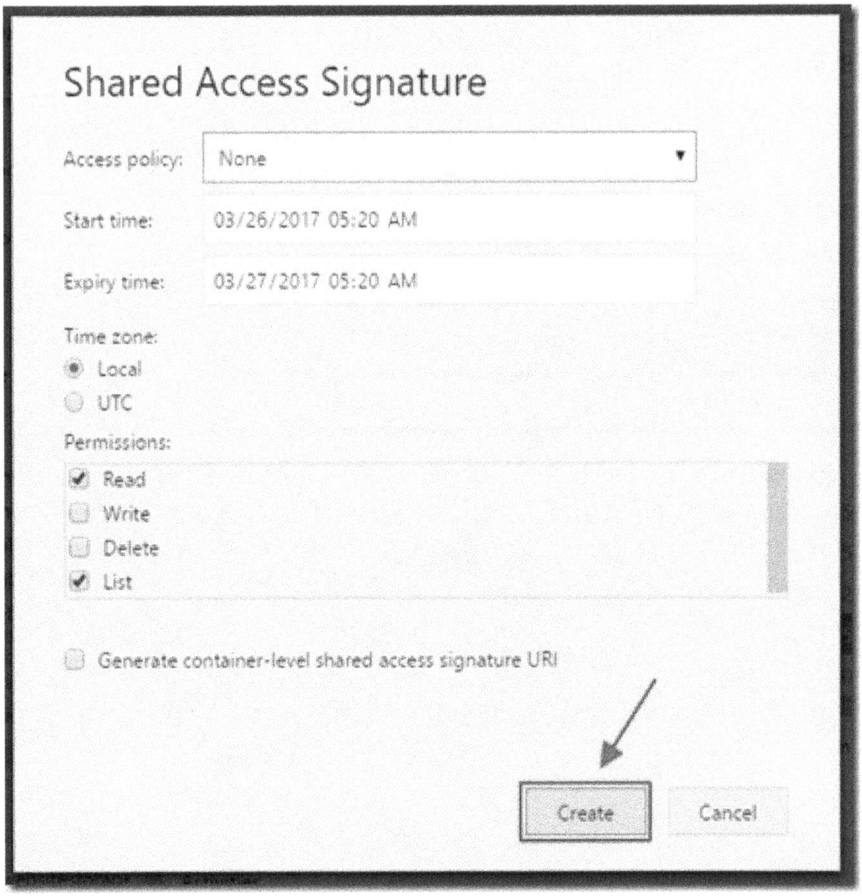

Click **Create**.

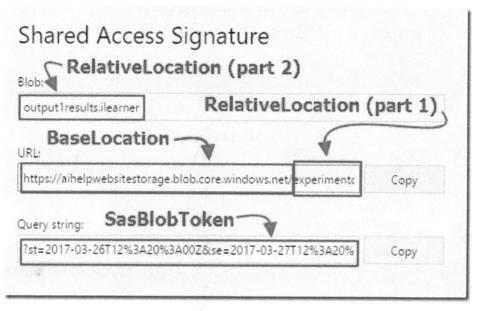

You can now retrieve the needed values.

Create New Endpoint
Patch and Consume Web Service

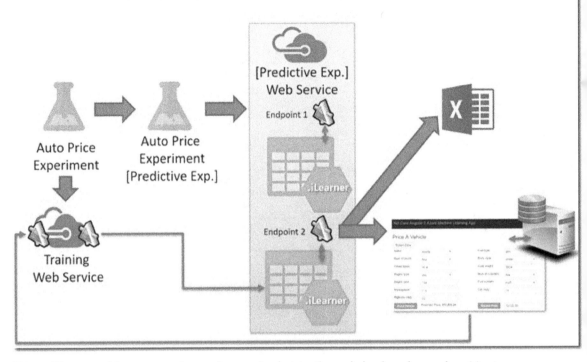

We will now add a new web service endpoint to the original web service (**Auto Price Experiment [Predictive Exp.]** <u>not</u> **Auto Price Experiment (Training)**) and perform a *patch* on that new endpoint to have it use the new *iLearner* **Model**.

We will then point the **Angular 2** application to this new endpoint.

Add A New Endpoint And Patch It

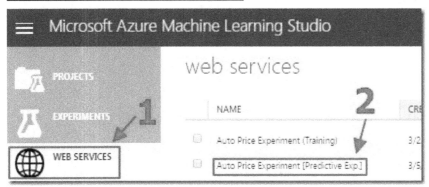

Log into the Azure Machine Learning Studio and select the **Auto Price Experiment [Predictive Exp.]**.

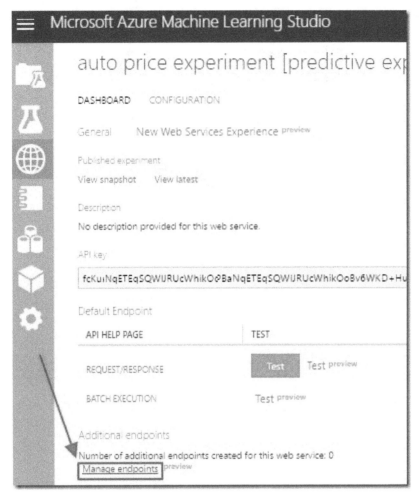

Click the **Manage endpoints** link.

← Classic Web Services

Auto Price Experiment [Predictive Exp.]

No description provided for this web service.

NAME	BATCH CALLS	FAILURES	SUCCESS RATE (%)	LAST USED	CREATED ON
default	0	0	0	03/05/2017 19:50 PM	03/05/2017 19:50 PM

Click the **New** button to create a new endpoint.

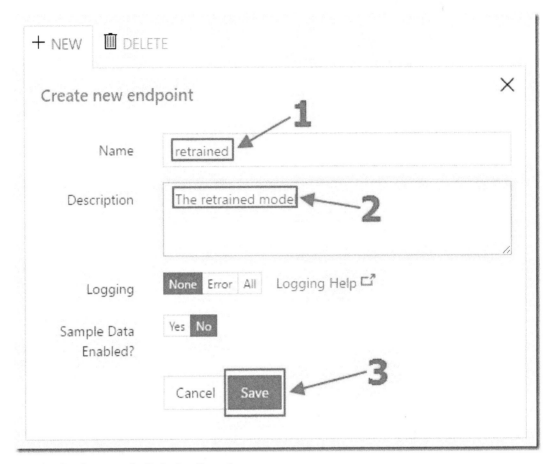

Fill in the form and click the **Save** button.

NAME	BATCH CALLS	FAILURES	SUCCESS RATE (%)	LAST USED	CREATED ON
default	0	0	0	03/05/2017 19:50 PM	03/05/2017 19:50 PM
retrained	0	0	0	03/26/2017 08:43 AM	03/26/2017 08:43 AM

1 ▼ / 1

The new endpoint will display.

Click on it to select it.

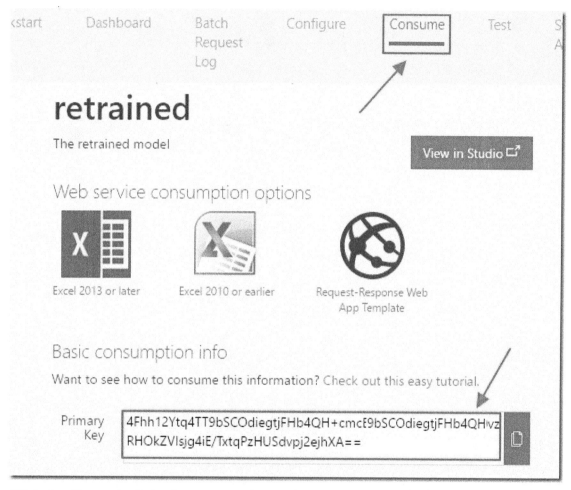

Click the **Consume** link, then *copy* and save the **Primary Key** (you will need it for the **API Key** in the **Patch service** created in the next steps).

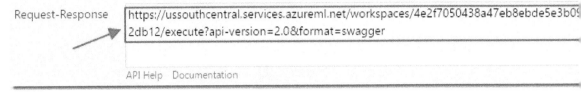

Also, *copy* and save the value in the **Request-Response** section (you will need it for the **BaseAddress** in the **Angular 2** application that we will update in the final step).

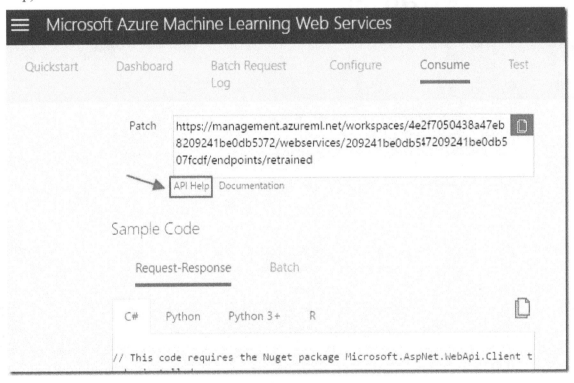

Scroll down to the **Patch** section and click the **API Help** link.

Update Resource API Documenta
Experiment [Predictive Exp.]

Updated: 03/06/2017 03:50

No description provided for this web service.

- Request and Response summary
- Sample Code
- API Swagger Document
- Endpoint Managment Swagger Document

Updatable Resources

Resource Name
Auto Price Experiment [trained model]

This will open the *Patch configuration* page.

Click the **Sample Code** link.

Sample Code

1

| C# | Python | R | **2** | Select sample code |

```
        {
            InvokeService().Wait();
        }

        static async Task InvokeService()
        {
            const string url = "https://management.azureml.net/workspaces/4e2f7050438a47eb8ebde5e3b0986
            const string apikey = "abc123"; // Replace this with the API key for the web service

            var resourceLocations = new ResourceLocations()
            {
                Resources = new ResourceLocation[] {
                    new ResourceLocation()
                    {
                        Name = "Auto Price Experiment [trained model]",
                        Location = new AzureBlobDataReference()
                        {
                            // Replace these values with the ones that specify the location of the new
                            // if this resource is a trained model, you must first execute the training
                            // to generate the new trained model. The location of the new trained model
                            // in the response.
                            BaseLocation = "https://somestorageaccount.blob.core.windows.net/",
                            RelativeLocation = "someblobcontainer/sometrainedmodel.ilearner",
                            SasBlobToken = "?sv=yyyy-mm-dd&sr=c&sig=somesignature&st=yyyy-mm-ddT20%3A31
                        }
                    }
```

Click the **C#** tab and copy the sample code.

Use **Visual Studio** to create a new console program.

```
51              {
52                  const string url = "https://management.azureml.net/workspa
53                  const string apiKey = "fcKu5EE170ygy1uXv9pVhkqd0PBaNqETEqS
54
55      ⊟       var resourceLocations = new ResourceLocations()
56      |       {
57      ⊟           Resources = new ResourceLocation[] {
58      ⊟               new ResourceLocation()
59      |               {
60                          Name = "Auto Price Experiment [trained model]"
61      ⊟                   Location = new AzureBlobDataReference()
62      |                   {
63                              // Replace these values with the ones that
64                              // if this resource is a trained model, yo
65                              // to generate the new trained model. The
66                              // in the response.
67                              BaseLocation = "https://aihelpwebsitestora
68                              RelativeLocation = "experimentoutput/outpu
69                              SasBlobToken = "?st=2017-03-26T15%3A03%3A0
70                          }
71                      }
72                  }
```

Follow the directions (that you will see in the code comments) to install the required assemblies.

Update the code with the values saved from the earlier steps.

*(Remember that **apiKey** is the **Primary Key** that we saved on the **Consume** page earlier.)*

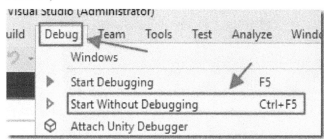

Run the application.

If a window opens for a few seconds then closes without showing any errors, this means the **Patch** worked.

Consume The New Endpoint

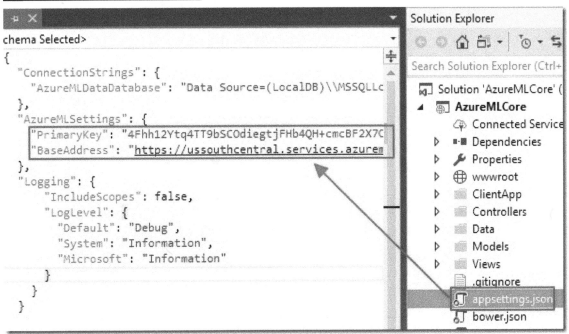

Open the **Angular 2** application, which we created in the previous chapter, in **Visual Studio**.

Open the **appsettings.json** file and update the **PrimaryKey** with the **PrimaryKey** you copied earlier and the **BaseAddress** with the **Request-Response** value you copied earlier.

However, with **BaseAddress**, change the ending of the value from:

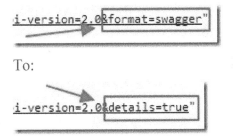

To:

i-version=2.0&details=true"

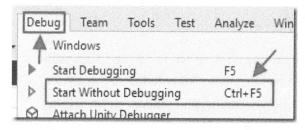

Run the application.

You will now be able to retrieve improved predictions.

About the Author

Michael Washington is an ASP.NET, C#, and Visual Basic programmer. He has extensive knowledge in process improvement, billing systems, and student information systems. He is a Microsoft MVP. He has a son, Zachary, and resides in Los Angeles with his wife, Valerie.

He has written several tutorials that are posted at http://AiHelpWebsite.com/Blog.

He is the author of seven previous books:

- **An Introduction to the Microsoft Bot Framework** (AiHelpWebsite.com)
- **Creating HTML 5 Websites and Cloud Business Apps Using LightSwitch In Visual Studio 2013-2015** (LightSwitchHelpWebsite.com)
- **Creating Web Pages Using the LightSwitch HTML Client In Visual Studio 2012** (LightSwitchHelpWebsite.com)
- **OData And Visual Studio LightSwitch** (LightSwitchHelpWebsite.com)
- **Creating Visual Studio LightSwitch Custom Controls (Beginner to Intermediate)** (LightSwitchHelpWebsite.com)
- **Building Websites with VB.NET and DotNetNuke 4** (Packt Publishing)
- **Building Websites with DotNetNuke 5** (Packt Publishing)

www.ingramcontent.com/pod-product-compliance
Lightning Source LLC
Chambersburg PA
CBHW080419060326
40689CB00019B/4296